Anonymus

Letters of the Right Honourable Lady Mary Wortley Montague

Anonymus

Letters of the Right Honourable Lady Mary Wortley Montague

ISBN/EAN: 9783741180378

Manufactured in Europe, USA, Canada, Australia, Japa

Cover: Foto ©Andreas Hilbeck / pixelio.de

Manufactured and distributed by brebook publishing software (www.brebook.com)

Anonymus

Letters of the Right Honourable Lady Mary Wortley Montague

LETTERS

OF THE

RIGHT HONOURABLE

LADY MARY WORTLEY

MONTAGUE.

A new edition, to which are now added
THE POETICAL WORKS of the
fame Lady.

IN FIVE VOLUMES.

VOL. III. IV. V.

LETTERS
OF THE
RIGHT HONOURABLE
LADY MARY WORTLEY
MONTAGUE.

Written during her TRAVELS in
EUROPE, ASIA AND AFRICA,
TO
Perſons of Diſtinction, Men of Letters,
etc. in different PARTS of EUROPE.

WHICH CONTAIN,
Among other CURIOUS Relations,
Accounts of the POLICY and MAN-
NERS of the TURKS,
Drawn from Sources that have been
inacceſſible to other Travellers.

VOL. III. IV. V.

VIENNA:
Printed for R. SAMMER, Bookſeller.
M. DCC. XCVII.

A SUMMARY of the CONTENTS OF THE LETTERS in the third VOLUME.

VOLUME III.

LETTER XLIII. from Constantinople.

OBSERVATIONS on the accounts given by Sir Paul Ricaut and Gemelli—the canal between Constantinople and Chalcedon—the precarious nature of human grandeur in Turkey—description of the house of the Grand Vizier who was killed at Peterwaradin—moral reflections on the difference between the taste of Europeans and the Easterns.

LETTER XLIV. from Tunis.

Voyage from Conſtantinople—the Hellespont, and caſtles of Seſtos and Abydos—reflections on the ſtory of Hero and Leander—the burial places of Hecuba and Achilles — antiquities — habits of the Greek peaſants—conjectures as to the ruins of a large city—remarks on the face of the country illuſtrated, by reference to paſſages from Homer— Troy, no remains of it exiſting—ruins of old Conſtantinople—Latin inſcriptions, and remains of antiquity—iſle of Tenedos—Mitylene—Leſbos—Scio and its inhabitants—promontory of Sunium, the preſent cape Colonna—temple of Theſeus, how deſtroyed—preſent condition of the Morea, the antient Peloponneſus—Candia—reflections on the contraſt between antient and modern Greece—Trinacria—Malta — arrival at Tunis — face of the country—manner of celebrating the Mahometan ramadan or Lent—the natives—ruins of the aqueduct of Carthage—defcription and chronological anecdotes of the city of Tunis—ruins of Carthage.

LETTER XLV. from Genoa.

Defcription of Genoa and its inhabitants—Cicifbeis, the nature of their employment, and occafion of their inftitution—the government—palaces—paintings—remark on their fondnefs for the reprefentation of crucifixes—church of St. Laurence, and the famous emerald plate—their churches not to be compared with Sancta Sophia at Conftantinople.

LETTER XLVI. from Turin.

Character of Turin, its palaces and churches—lady M. waits on the Queen—perfons of the King and Prince of Piedmont defcribed.

viii

LETTER XLVII. from Lyons.

Journey from Turin to Lyons—paſſage over mount Cenis — the frontier towns between Savoy and France.

LETTER XLVIII. Lyons.

Reflections on the inſipidity of female viſits — the inſcriptions on braſs tables on each ſide of the town-houſe at Lyons — remains of antiquity—cathedral of St. John — critique on the ſtatue of Louis XIV.

LETTER XLIX. from Paris.

Miſerable condition of the French peaſants—palace of Fontainbleau — fair of St. Laurence — Opera houſe — general character of the French actors—compariſon between the French and Engliſh ladies.

LETTER L. Paris.

General remarks on the palace of Versailles — Trianon — Marli — St. Cloud — paintings at the house of the duke D'Antin — the Thuilleries — the Louvre — behaviour of Mr. Law at Paris — Paris compared with London.

LETTER LI. from Dover,

Ludicrous distresses in the passage to Dover — reflections on travelling — brief comparison between England and the rest of the world in general.

LETTER LII. Dover.

Reflections on the fates of John Hughes and Sarah Drew — epitaph on them.

VOLUME IV.

Letter LIII.

Character of Mrs. D—— and humorous representation of her intended marriage with a greasy curate——anecdotes of another couple—remarks on the abuse of the word *nature*, applied to the case of a husband who insisted on his wife suckling her own child—observations on the forbidding countenance of a worthy gentleman.

Letter LIV. from Vienna.

Remarks on some illustrious Personages at the court of Vienna—character of the poet Rousseau—alchymy much studied at Vienna—prince Eugene's library.

LETTER LV.

Victory of prince Eugene over the Turks, and the furrender of Belgrade—the news how received at Conftantinople—contraft between European and Afiatic manners—eftimate of the pleafures of the feraglio—obfervations on Mr. Addifon being appointed Secretary of State—Mr. Addifon, Mr. Pope and Mr. Congreve, in what refpect three happy poets—reflections on the Iliad, and Mr. Pope's tranflation of it.

LETTER LVI. from Florence.

Remarks on the road between Bologna and Florence—vifit to the monaftery of La Trappe, with reflections on the monaftic life—occafion of the inftitution of the order of La Trappe—the burning mountains near Firenzuola—general defcription of Florence—the Grand gallery—the ftatues of Antinous and Venus de

Medicis—the first sketches of Raphael's cartoons — envious behaviour of modern painters in defacing the productions of the antients—digression to some reports raised by Mr. P. concerning the writer.

Letter LVII.

Remarks on Paris—reflections on staring and grinning—character of the French people—criticism on statues in the gardens of Versailles—the gardens compared with the royal gardens of England.

Letter LVIII.

Observations on the Koran, and the conduct of the Greek priests with regard to it—women not excluded from Mahomet's paradise—who among the women excluded—the exhortations of Mahomet to the women, compared with the monastic institution of popery—the sciences cultivated among the Turks by the Effendis—sentiments of an intelligent one respecting abstinence from wine—strange mixture of different countries in the suburbs of Constantinople—different species of men asserted—mungrels in the human species—why the English women so fond of hoop petticoats.

Inquiry into the truth of Monsieur Rochefoucault's maxim: „That marriage is sometimes convenient, but never deightful."

Verses written in the Chiosk at Pera verlooking Constantinople, December 6, 1718. By Lady Mary Wortley Montague.

Verses to the Lady Mary Wortley Montague. By Mr. Pope.

LETTERS

OF THE

RIGHT HONOURABLE

LADY MARY WORTLEY

MONTAGUE.

VOLUME III.

LETTER XLIII.

To the Abbot of ———.

Constantinople, May 19. 1718.

I AM extremely pleased with hearing from you, and my vanity (the darling frailty of human kind) not a little flattered by the uncommon questions you ask me, though I am utterly incapable of answering them. And, indeed, were I as good a mathematician as Euclid himself, it requires an age's stay to make just observations on the air and vapours. I have not been yet a full year here, and am on the point of removing. Such is my rambling destiny. This will surprise you, and can surprise no body so much as myself. Perhaps, you will accuse me of laziness, or dulness, or both together, that can leave this place, without giving you some account of the Turkish court. I can only tell you, that if you please to read Sir Paul Rycaut, you will there find a full and true account of the Viziers, the *Beglerbies*, the civil and spiritual government, the officers of the seraglio, etc. things that 'tis very easy to procure lists of, and therefore may be depended on; though other stories, God knows——I say no more ——every body is at liberty to write their own remarks; the manners of people may change, or some of them escape the observation of travellers; but 'tis not the same of the government; and, for that reason, since I can tell you nothing new, I will tell you nothing of it. In the same silence shall be passed over the arsenal and seven towers; and for mosques, I have already described one of the noblest to you very particularly. But I cannot forbear taking notice to you of a mistake of Gemelli, (though I honour him in a much higher degree than any other voyage-writer:) he says that there are no remains of Chalcedon; this is certainly a mistake: I was there yesterday, and went cross the canal in my galley, the sea being very narrow between that city and Constantinople. 'Tis still a large town, and has several mosques in it. The Christians still call it Chalcedonia, and the Turks give it a name I forgot, but which is only a corruption of the same word. I suppose this is an error of his guide, which his short stay hindered him from rectifying; for I have, in other matters, a very just esteem for his veracity. Nothing can be pleasanter than the canal; and the Turks are so well acquainted with its beauties, that all their pleasure-seats are built on its banks, where they have, at the same time, the most beautiful prospects in Europe and Asia; there are, near one another, some hundreds of magnificent palaces. Human grandeur being here yet more unstable than any where else, 'tis common for the heirs of a great three-tailed Baſſa, not to be rich enough to keep in repair the houſe he built; thus, in a few years, they all fall to ruin. I was yeſterday to ſee that of the late Grand Vizier, who was killed at Peterwaradin. It was built to receive his royal bride, daughter of the preſent Sultan; but he did not live to ſee her there. I have a great mind to deſcribe it to you; but I check that inclination, knowing very well, that I cannot give you, with my beſt deſcription, ſuch an idea of it as I ought. It is ſituated on one of the moſt delightful parts of the canal, with a fine wood on the ſide of a hill behind it. The extent of it is prodigious; the guardian aſſured me, there are eight hundred rooms in it; I will not, however, anſwer for that number, ſince I did not count them; but 'tis certain the number is very large, and the whole adorned with a profusion of marble, gilding, and the most exquisite painting of fruit and flowers. The windows are all sashed with the finest chrystalline glass brought from England; and here is all the expensive magnificence that you can suppose in a palace founded by a vain luxurious young man, with the wealth of a vast empire at his command. But no part of it pleased me better than the apartments destined for the bagnios. There are two built exactly in the same manner, answering to one another; the baths, fountains, and pavements, all of white marble, the roofs gilt, and the walls covered with Japan china. Adjoining to them are two rooms, the uppermost of which is divided into a sofa, and in the four corners are falls of water from the very roof, from shell to shell, of white marble, to the lower end of the room, where it falls into a large basin, surrounded with pipes, that throw up the water as high as the roof. The walls are in the nature of lattices; and, on the outfide of them, there are vines and woodbines planted, that form a fort of green tapeftry, and give an agreeable obfcurity to thofe delightful chambers. I fhould go on and let you into fome of the other apartments (all worthy your curiofity) but 'tis yet harder to defcribe a Turkifh palace than any other, being built entirely irregular. There is nothing that can be properly called front or wings; and though fuch a confufion is, I think, pleafing to the fight, yet it would be very unintelligible in a letter. I fhall only add, that the chamber deftined for the Sultan, when he vifits his daughter, is wainfcotted with mother of pearl, faftened with emeralds like nails. There are others of mother of pearl and olive wood inlaid, and feveral of Japan china. The galleries, which are numerous, and very large, are adorned with jars of flowers, and porcelain dishes of fruit of all sorts, so well done in plaister, and coloured in so lively a manner, that it has an enchanting effect. The garden is suitable to the house, where arbours, fountains, and walks, are thrown together in an agreeable confusion. There is no ornament wanting, except that of statues. Thus, you see, Sir, these people are not so unpolished as we represent them. 'Tis true, their magnificence is of a different taste from ours, and perhaps of a better. I am almost of opinion, they have a right notion of life. They consume it in music, gardens, wine, and delicate eating, while we are tormenting our brains with some scheme of politics, or studying some science to which we can never attain, or, if we do, cannot persuade other people to set that value upon it we do ourselves. 'Tis certain, what we feel and see is properly (if any thing is properly) our own; but the good of fame, the folly of praife, are hardly purchafed, and, when obtained, a poor recompenfe for lofs of time and health. We die or grow old before we can reap the fruit of our labours. Confidering what fhort-lived, weak animals men are, is there any ftudy fo beneficial as the ftudy of prefent pleafure? I dare not purfue this theme; perhaps I have already faid too much, but I depend upon the true knowledge you have of my heart. I don't expect from you the infipid railleries I fhould fuffer from another in anfwer to this letter. You know how to divide the idea of *pleafure* from that of *vice*, and they are only mingled in the heads of fools.——But I allow you to laugh at me for the fenfual declaration in faying, that I had rather be a rich *Effendi*, with all his ignorance, than Sir Ifaac Newton with all his knowledge.

      I am, Sir, etc. etc.

LETTER XLIV.

To the Abbot of ——.

Tunis, July 31. 1718.

I LEFT Conſtantinople the ſixth of the laſt month, and this is the firſt poſt from whence I could ſend a letter, though I have often wiſhed for the opportunity, that I might impart ſome of the pleaſure I found in this voyage, through the moſt agreeable part of the world, where every ſcene preſents me ſome poetical idea.

Warm'd with poetic tranſport I ſurvey
Th' immortal iſlands, and the well known ſea.
For here ſo oft the muſe her harp has ſtrung,
That not a mountain rears its head unſung.

I beg your pardon for this ſally, and will, if I can, continue the reſt of my account in plain proſe. The ſecond day after we set sail, we passed Gallipolis, a fair city, situated in the bay of Cherfonefus, and much respected by the Turks, being the first town they took in Europe. At five the next morning, we anchored in the Hellespont, between the castles of Sestos and Abydos, now called the Dardanelli. These are now two little ancient castles, but of no strength, being commanded by a rising ground behind them, which I confess I should never have taken notice of, if I had not heard it observed by our captain and officers, my imagination being wholly employed by the tragic story, that you are well acquainted with:

The swimming lover, and the nightly bride,
How *Hero* lov'd, and how *Leander* died.

Verse again!—I am certainly infected by the poetical air I have passed through. That of Abydos is undoubtedly very amorous, fince that foft paffion betrayed the caftle into the hands of the Turks who befieged it in the reign of Orchanes. The governour's daughter imagining to have feen her future hufband in a dream (though I don't find fhe had either flept upon bride-cake, or kept St. Agnes's faft) fancied fhe faw the dear figure in the form of one of her befiegers; and, being willing to obey her deftiny, toffed a note to him over the wall, with the offer of her perfon, and the delivery of the caftle. He fhewed it to his general, who confented to try the fincerity of her intentions, and withdrew his army, ordering the young man to return with a felect body of men at midnight. She admitted him at the appointed hour, he deftroyed the garrifon, took the father prifoner, and made her his wife. This town is in Afia, firft founded by the Milefians. Seftos is in Europe, and was once the principal city of Cherfonefus.

Since I have seen this strait, I find nothing improbable in the adventure of Leander, or very wonderful in the bridge of boats of Xerxes. 'Tis so narrow, 'tis not surprising a young lover should attempt to swim, or an ambitious King try to pass his army over it. But then, 'tis so subject to storms, 'tis no wonder the lover perished, and the bridge was broken. From hence we had a full view of mount Ida;

Where Juno once caress'd her am'rous Jove,
And the world's master lay subdu'd by love.

Not many leagues sail from hence, I saw the point of land where poor old Hecuba was buried, and about a league from that place is Cape Janizary, the famous promontory of Sigaeum, where we anchored. My curiosity supplied me with strength to climb to the top of it, to see the place where Achilles was buried, and where Alexander ran naked round his tomb, in honour of him, which, no doubt, was a great comfort to his ghost. I saw there, the ruins of a very large city, and found a stone, on which Mr. Wortley plainly distinguished the words of *Sigaen Polin.* We ordered this on board the ship, but were shewed others much more curious, by a Greek priest, tho' a very ignorant fellow, that could give no tolerable account of any thing. On each side the door of this little church lie two large stones, about ten feet long each, five in breadth, and three in thickness. That on the right is a very fine white marble, the side of it beautifully carved in bas-relief; it represents a woman, who seems to be designed for some deity, sitting on a chair with a footstool, and before her another woman, weeping, and presenting to her a young child that she has in her arms, followed by a proceſſion of women with children in the ſame manner. This is certainly part of a very ancient tomb; but I dare not pretend to give the true explanation of it. On the ſtone, on the left ſide, is a very fair inſcription; but the Greek is too ancient for Mr. Wortley's interpretation. I am very ſorry not to have the original in my poſſeſſion, which might have been purchaſed of the poor inhabitants for a ſmall ſum of money. But our captain aſſured us, that, without having machines made on purpoſe, 'twas impoſſible to bear it to the ſea-ſide, and, when it was there, his long-boat would not be large enough to hold it.

The ruins of this great city are now inhabited by poor Greek peaſants, who wear the Sciote habit, the women being in ſhort petticoats, faſtened by ſtraps round their ſhoulders, and large ſmock ſleeves of white linen, with neat ſhoes and flockings, and on their heads a large piece of muflin, which falls in large folds on their fhoulders.—One of my countrymen, Mr. Sands, (whofe book I doubt not you have read, as one of the beft of its kind) fpeaking of thefe ruins, fuppofes them to have been the foundation of a city begun by Conftantine, before his building Byzantium; but I fee no good reafon for that imagination, and am apt to believe them much more ancient.

We faw very plainly from this promontory, the river Simois rolling from mount Ida, and running through a very fpacious valley. It is now a confiderable river, and is called Simores; it is joined in the vale by the Scamander, which appeared a fmall ftream half choked with mud, but is perhaps large in the winter. This was Xanthus amongft the gods, as Homer tells us; and 'tis by that heavenly name, the nymph Oenone invokes it, in her epistle to Paris. The Trojan virgins used to offer their first favours to it, by the name of Scamander, till the adventure, which Monsieur de la Fontaine has told so agreeably, abolished that heathenish ceremony. When the stream is mingled with the Simois, they run together to the sea.

All that is now left of Troy is the ground on which it stood; for, I am firmly persuaded, whatever pieces of antiquity may be found round it, are much more modern, and I think Strabo says the same thing. However, there is some pleasure in seeing the valley where I imagined the famous duel of Menelaus and Paris had been fought, and where the greatest city in the world was situated. 'Tis certainly the noblest situation that can be found for the head of a great empire, much to be preferred to that of Constantinople, the harbour here being always convenient for ships from all parts of the world, and that of Conſtantinople inacceſſible almoſt ſix months in the year, while the north-wind reigns.

North of the promontory of Sigaeum we ſaw that of Rhaeteum, famed for the ſepulchre of Ajax. While I viewed theſe celebrated fields and rivers, I admired the exact geography of Homer, whom I had in my hand. Almoſt every epithet he gives to a mountain or plain, is ſtill juſt for it; and I ſpent ſeveral hours here in as agreeable cogitations, as ever Don Quixote had on mount Monteſinos. We ſailed next night to the ſhore, where 'tis vulgarly reported Troy ſtood; and I took the pains of riſing at two in the morning to view cooly thoſe ruins which are commonly ſhewed to ſtrangers, and which the Turks call *Eſki Stamboul*, i. e. Old Conſtantinople. For that reaſon, as well as ſome others, I conjecture them to be the remains of that city begun by Conſtantine. I hired an aſs (the only voiture to be had there) that I might go some miles into the country, and take a tour round the ancient walls, which are of a vast extent. We found the remains of a castle on a hill, and of another in a valley, several broken pillars and two pedestals, from which I took these Latin inscriptions:

DIVI. AUG. COL.
ET. COL. IUL. PHILIPPENSIS.
EORUNDEM. ET. PRINCIP. AM.
COL. IUL. PARIANAE. TRIBUN.
MILIT. COH. XXXII. VOLUNTAR.
TRIB. MILIT. LEG. XIII. GEM.
PRAEFECTO. EQUIT. ALAE. I.
SCUBULORUM.
VIC. VIII.

DIVI. IULI. FLAMINI.
C. ANTONIO. M. F.
VOLT. RUFO. FLAMIN.
DIV. AUG. COL. CL. APRENS.

ET. COL. IUL. PHILIPPENSIS.
EORUNDEM. ET. PRINCIP. ITEM.
COL. IUL. FABIANAE. TRIB.
MILIT. COH. XXXII. VOLUNTARIOR.
TRIB. MILIT. XIII.
GEM. PRAEF. EQUIT. ALAE. I.
SCUBULORUM.
VIC. VII.

I do not doubt but the remains of a temple near this place, are the ruins of one dedicated to Auguſtus; and I know not why Mr. Sands calls it a Chriſtian temple, ſince the Romans certainly built hereabouts. Here are many tombs of fine marble, and vaſt pieces of granate, which are daily leſſened by the prodigious balls that the Turks make from them, for their cannon. We paſſed that evening the iſle of Tenedos, once under the patronage of Apollo, as he gave it in, himſelf, in the particulars of his eſtate, when he courted Daphne. It is but ten miles in circuit, but, in thofe days, very rich and well peopled, ftill famous for its excellent wine. I fay nothing of Tenes, from whom it was called; but naming Mitylene, where we paffed next, I cannot forbear mentioning Lefbos, where Sappho fung, and Pittacus reigned, famous for the birth of Alcaeus, Theophraftus and Arion, thofe mafters in poetry, philofophy, and mufick. This was one of the laft iflands that remained in the Chriftian dominion after the conqueft of Conftantinople by the Turks. But need I talk to you of Catucufeno, etc. princes that you are as well acquainted with as I am? 'Twas with regret I faw us fail from this ifland into the Egean fea, now the Archipelago, leaving Scio (the ancient Chios) on the left, which is the richeft and moft populous of thefe iflands, fruitful in cotton, corn and filk, planted with groves of orange and lemon trees, and the Arvifian mountain, ſtill celebrated for the nectar that Virgil mentions. Here is the beſt manufacture of ſilks in all Turkey. The town is well built; the women famous for their beauty, and ſhew their faces as in Chriſtendom. There are many rich families; though they confine their magnificence to the inſide of their houſes, to avoid the jealouſy of the Turks, who have a Baſſa here: however, they enjoy a reaſonable liberty, and indulge the genius of their country;

And eat, and ſing, and dance away their time,
Freſh as their groves, and happy as their clime.

Their chains hang lightly on them, tho' 'tis not long ſince they were impoſed, not being under the Turk till 1566. But perhaps 'tis as eaſy to obey the Grand Signior as the ſtate of Genoa, to whom they were ſold by the Greek Emperor.

But I forget myself in these historical touches, which are very impertinent when I write to you. Passing the strait between the islands of Andros and Achaia, now Libadia, we saw the promontory of Sunium, now called Cape Colonna, where are yet standing the vast pillars of a temple of Minerva. This venerable sight made me think, with double regret, on a beautiful temple of Theseus, which I am assured, was almost entire at Athens, till the last campaign in the Morea, that the Turks filled it with powder, and it was accidentally blown up. You may believe I had a great mind to land on the famed Peloponnesus, tho' it were only to look on the rivers of Asopus, Peneus, Inachus and Eurotas, the fields of Arcadia, and other scenes of ancient mythology. But instead of demi-gods and heroes, I was credibly informed, 'tis now overrun by robbers, and that I should run a great risque of falling into their hands, by undertaking such a journey through a desert country, for which, however, I have so much respect, that I have much ado to hinder myself from troubling you with its whole history, from the foundation of Nycana and Corinth, to the last campaign there; but I check the inclination as I did that of landing. We sailed quietly by Cape Angelo, once Malea, where I saw no remains of the famous temple of Apollo. We came that evening in sight of Candia; it is very mountainous; we easily distinguished that of Ida.—We have Virgil's authority, that here were a hundred cities—

—Centum urbes habitant magnas—

The chief of them—the scene of monstrous passions.——Metellus first conquered this birth-place of his Jupiter; it fell afterwards into the hands of——I am running on to the very siege of Candia; and I am so angry with myself, that I will pass by all the other islands with this general reflection, that 'tis impossible to imagine any thing more agreeable than this journey would have been two or three thousand years since, when, after drinking a dish of tea with Sappho, I might have gone, the same evening, to visit the temple of Homer in Chios, and passed this voyage in taking plans of magnificent temples, delineating the miracles of statuaries, and conversing with the most polite and most gay of mankind. Alas! art is extinct here; the wonders of nature alone remain; and it is with vast pleasure I observed those of mount Aetna, whose flame appears very bright in the night many leagues off at sea, and fills the head with a thousand conjectures. However, I honour philosophy too much, to imagine it could turn that of Empedocles; and Lucian shall never make me believe such a scandal of a man, of whom Lucretius says,

—Vix humana videtur stirpe creatus.—

We passed Trinacria without hearing any of the syrens that Homer describes, and, being thrown on neither Scylla nor Charybdis, came safe to Malta, first called Melita, from the abundance of honey. It is a whole rock covered with very little earth. The Grand Master lives here in the state of a sovereign prince; but his strength at sea now is very small. The fortifications are reckoned the best in the world, all cut in the solid rock with infinite expence and labour.— — Off this island we were tossed by a severe storm, and were very glad, after eight days, to be able to put into Porta Farine on the African shore, where our ship now rides. At Tunis we were met by the English consul who resides here. I readily accepted of the offer of his house there for some days, being very curious to see this part of the world, and particularly the ruins of Carthage. I set out in his chaise at nine at night, the moon being at full. I saw the prospect of the country almost as well as I could have done by daylight; and the heat of the sun is now so intolerable, 'tis impossible to travel at any other time. The soil is, for the most part, sandy, but every where fruitful of date, olive, and fig-trees, which grow without art, yet afford the most delicious fruit in the world. Their vineyards and melon-fields are inclos'd by hedges of that plant we call Indian fig, which is an admirable fence, no wild beast being able to pass it. It grows a great height, very thick, and the spikes or thorns are as long and sharp as bodkins; it bears a fruit much eaten by the peasants, and which has no ill taste.

It being now the season of the Turkish

ramadan, or Lent, and all here professing, at least, the Mahometan religion, they fast till the going down of the sun, and spend the night in feasting. We saw under the trees, companies of the country people, eating, singing, and dancing, to their wild music. They are not quite black, but all mulattoes, and the most frightful creatures that can appear in a human figure. They are almost naked, only wearing a piece of coarse serge wrapped about them.——But the women have their arms, to their very shoulders, and their necks and faces, adorned with flowers, stars, and various sorts of figures impressed by gun-powder; a considerable addition to their natural deformity; which is, however, esteemed very ornamental amongst them; and I believe they suffer a good deal of pain by it.

About six miles from Tunis, we saw the remains of that noble aqueduct, which carried the water to Carthage, over several high mountains, the length of forty miles. There are still many arches entire. We spent two hours viewing it with great attention, and Mr. Wortley assured me that of Rome is very much inferior to it. The stones are of a prodigious size, and yet all polished, and so exactly fitted to each other, very little cement has been made use of to join them. Yet they may probably stand a thousand years longer, if art is not made use of to pull them down. Soon after day-break I arrived at Tunis, a town fairly built of very white stone, but quite without gardens, which, they say, were all destroyed when the Turks first took it, none having been planted since. The dry land gives a very disagreeable prospect to the eye; and the want of shade contributing to the natural heat of the climate, renders it so excessive, that I have much ado to support it. 'Tis true

here is, every noon, the refreshment of
the sea-breeze, without which it would
be impossible to live; but no fresh water
but what is preserved in the cisterns of
the rains that fall in the month of September. The women of the town go veiled from head to foot under a black crape,
and being mixed with a breed of renegadoes, are said to be many of them fair
and handsome. This city was besieged
in 1270, by Lewis King of France, who
died under the walls of it, of a pestilential fever. After his death, Philip, his
son, and our prince Edward, son of
Henry III. raised the siege on honourable
terms. It remained under its natural African kings, till betrayed into the hands
of Barbarossa, admiral of Solyman the
Magnificent. The Emperor Charles V.
expelled Barbarossa, but it was recovered by the Turk, under the conduct
of Sinan Bassà, in the reign of Selim II.
From that time till now, it has remain-

ed tributary to the Grand Signior, governed by a *Bey*, who suffers the name of subject to the Turk, but has renounced the subjection, being absolute, and very seldom paying any tribute. The great city of Bagdat is, at this time, in the same circumstances; and the Grand Signior connives at the loss of these dominions, for fear of losing even the titles of them.

I went very early yesterday morning (after one night's repose) to see the ruins of Carthage.——I was, however, half broiled in the sun, and overjoyed to be led into one of the subterranean apartments, which they called, *The stables of the elephants*, but which I cannot believe were ever designed for that use. I found in many of them broken pieces of columns of fine marble, and some of porphyry. I cannot think any body would take the insignificant pains of carrying them thither, and I cannot imagine such

fine pillars were defigned for the ufe of
ftables. I am apt to believe they were
fummer apartments under their palaces,
which the heat of the climate rendered
necefſary. They are now uſed as grana-
ries by the country people. While I fat
here, from the town of *Tents* not far
off, many of the women flocked in to
fee me, and we were equally entertained with viewing one another. Their pof-
ture in fitting, the colour of their fkin,
their lank black hair falling on each fide
their faces, their features, and the fhape
of their limbs, differ fo little from their
country-people the baboons, 'tis hard to
fancy them a diftinct race; I could not
help thinking there had been fome ancient alliances between them.

When I was a little refrefhed by reft,
and fome milk and exquifite fruit they
brought me, I went up the little hill
where once flood the caftle of Byrfa,
and from thence I had a diftinct view of

the fituation of the famous city of Carthage, which flood on an ifthmus, the fea coming on each fide of it. 'Tis now a marfhy ground on one fide, where there are falt ponds. Strabo calls Carthage forty miles in circumference. There are now no remains of it, but what I have defcribed; and the hiftory of it is too well known to want any abridgement of it. You fee, Sir, that I think you efteem obedience better than compliments. I have anfwered your letter, by giving you the accounts you defired, and have referved my thanks to the conclufion. I intend to leave this place to-morrow, and continue my journey through Italy and France. In one of thofe places I hope to tell you, by word of mouth, that I am,

   Your humble fervant, etc. etc.

LETTER XLV.

To the Countess of ———.

Genoa, Aug. 28. 1718.

I BEG your pardon, my dear fifter, that I did not write to you from Tunis, the only opportunity I have had fince I left Conftantinople. But the heat there was fo excelfive, and the light fo bad for the fight, I was half blind by writing one letter to the Abbot ———; and durft not go to write many others I had defigned; nor indeed could I have entertained you very well out of that barbarous country. I am now furrounded with fubjects of pleafure, and fo much charmed with the beauties of Italy, that I fhould think it a kind of ingratitude not to offer a little praife in return for the diverfion I have had here.———I am in the houfe of Mrs. D'Avenant at St. Pierre d'Arena, and fhould be very unjuſt, not to allow her a ſhare of that praiſe I ſpeak of, ſince her good humour and good company have very much contributed to render this place agreeable to me.

Genoa is ſituated in a very fine bay; and being built on a riſing hill, intermixed with gardens, and beautified with the moſt excellent architecture, gives a very fine proſpect off at ſea; though it loſt much of its beauty in my eyes, having been accuſtomed to that of Conſtantinople. The Genoeſe were once maſters of ſeveral iſlands in the Archipelago, and all that part of Conſtantinople, which is now called Galata. Their betraying the Chriſtian cauſe, by facilitating the taking of Conſtantinople by the Turk, deſerved what has ſince happened to them, even the loſs of all their conqueſts on that ſide to thoſe infidels. They are at preſent far from being rich, and are deſpiſed by the French, ſince their doge was forced by the late King to go in perſon to Paris, to aſk pardon for ſuch a trifle as the arms of France over the houſe of the envoy, being ſpattered with dung in the night. This I ſuppoſe; was done by ſome of the Spaniſh faction; which ſtill makes up the majority here, though they dare not openly declare it. The ladies affect the French habit, and are more genteel than thoſe they imitate. I do not doubt but the cuſtom of Ciziſbei's has very much improved their airs. I know not whether you ever heard of thoſe animals. Upon my word, nothing but my own eyes could have convinced me there were any ſuch upon earth. The faſhion began here, and is now received all over Italy, where the huſbands are not ſuch terrible creatures as we repreſent them. There are none among them ſuch brutes, as to pretend to find fault with a cuſtom ſo well eſtabliſhed, and ſo politically founded.

since I am assured, that it was an expedient, first found out by the senate, to put an end to those family hatreds, which tore their state to pieces, and to find employment for those young men, who were forced to cut one another's throats, *pour passer le temps:* and it has succeeded so well, that since the institution of Cizisbei's, there has been nothing but peace and good humour amongst them. These are gentlemen who devote themselves to the service of a particular lady, (I mean a married one; for the virgins are all invisible and confined to convents.) They are obliged to wait on her to all public places, such as the plays, operas, and assemblies, (which are called here *Conversations*) where they wait behind her chair, take care of her fan and gloves; if she plays, have the privilege of whispers, etc.— —When she goes out, they serve her instead of lacquies, gravely trotting by her chair. 'Tis their bufinefs to prepare for her a prefent againſt any day of public appearance, not forgetting that of her own name *); in ſhort, they are to ſpend all their time and money in her fervice, who rewards them accordingly (for opportunity they want none); but the huſband is not to have the impudence to ſuppoſe this any other than pure Platonic friendſhip. 'Tis true, they endeavour to give her a Ciziſbeo of their own chuſing; but when the lady happens not to be of the fame taſte, as that often happens, ſhe never fails to bring it about to have one of her own fancy. In former times, one beauty uſed to have eight or ten of theſe humble admirers; but thoſe days of plenty and humility are no more. Men grow more fcarce and faucy, and every lady is forced to content herſelf with one at a time.

*) That is, the day of the Saint after whom ſhe is called.

D 2

You may see in this place the *glorious liberty* of a republic, or more properly, an aristocracy, the common people being here as arrant slaves as the French; but the old nobles pay little respect to the doge, who is but two years in his office, and whose wife, at that very time, assumes no rank above another noble lady. 'Tis true, the family of Andrea Doria (that great man, who restored them that liberty they enjoy) have some particular privileges. When the senate found it necessary to put a stop to the luxury of dress, forbidding the wearing of jewels and brocades, they left them at liberty to make what expence they pleased. I look with great pleasure on the statue of that hero, which is in the court belonging to the house of Duke Doria. This puts me in mind of their palaces, which I can never describe as I ought.——Is it not enough, that I say, they are, most of them, the design of

Palladio? The street called Strada Nuova, is perhaps the most beautiful line of buildings in the world. I must particularly mention the vast palaces of Durazzo, those of the two Balbi, joined together by a magnificent colonade, that of the Imperiale at this village of St. Pierre d'Arena, and another of the Doria. The perfection of architecture, and the utmost profusion of rich furniture are to be seen here, disposed with the most elegant taste, and lavish magnificence. But I am charmed with nothing so much as the collection of pictures by the pencils of Raphael, Paulo Veronese, Titian, Caracci, Michael Angelo, Guido, and Corregio, which two I mention last as my particular favourites. I own, I can find no pleasure in objects of horrour; and, in my opinion, the more naturally a crucifix is represented, the more disagreeable it is. These, my beloved painters, shew nature, and shew it in the moſt charming light. I was particularly pleaſed with a Lucretia in the houſe of Balbi; the expreſſive beauty of that face and boſom, gives all the paſſion of pity and admiration, that could be raiſed in the ſoul, by the fineſt poem on that ſubject. A Cleopatra of the ſame hand, deſerves to be mentioned; and I ſhould ſay more of her, if Lucretia had not firſt engaged my eyes.—Here are alſo ſome ineſtimable ancient buſtos.—The church of St. Laurence is built of black and white marble, where is kept that famous plate of a ſingle emerald, which is not now permitted to be handled, ſince a plot, which, they ſay, was diſcovered, to throw it on the pavement and break it; a childiſh piece of malice, which they aſcribe to the King of Sicily, to be revenged for their refuſing to ſell it to him. The church of the Annunciation is finely lined with marble; the pillars are of red and white marble;

that of St. Ambrofe has been very much
adorned by the Jefuits; but, I confefs,
all the churches appeared fo mean to
me, after that of Sancta Sophia, I can
hardly do them the honour of writing
down their names. But I hope you will
own, I have made good ufe of my time,
in feeing fo much, fince 'tis not many
days that we have been out of the qua-
rantine, from which no body is exempt-
ed coming from the Levant. Ours, indeed, was very much fhortened, and
very agreeably paffed in Mrs. D'Avenant's company, in the village of St.
Pierre d'Arena, about a mile from Genoa, in a houfe built by Palladio, fo
well defigned, and fo nobly proportion-
ed, 'twas a pleafure to walk in it. We
were vifited here only by a few Eng-
lifh, in the company of a noble Genoefe,
commiffioned to fee we did not touch
one another.——I fhall ftay here fome
days longer, and could almoft wifh it

were for all my life; but mine, I fear, is not destined to so much tranquillity.

I am, etc. etc.

LETTER XLVI.

To the Countess of ———.

Turin, Sept. 12. 1718.

I CAME in two days from Genoa, through fine roads, to this place. I have already seen what is shewed to strangers in the town, which, indeed, is not worth a very particular description; and I have not respect enough for the holy handkerchief, to speak long of it. The churches are handsome, and so is the King's palace; but I have lately seen such perfection of architecture, I did not give much of my attention to these pieces. The town itself is fairly built, situated in a fine plain on the banks of the Po. At a little distance from it, we saw the palaces of La Venerie, and La Valentin, both very agreeable retreats. We were lodged in the Piazza Royale, which is one of the nobleſt ſquares I ever ſaw, with a fine portico of white ſtone quite round it. We were immediately viſited by the Chevalier ———, whom you knew in England, who, with great civility, begged to introduce us at court, which is now kept at Rivoli, about a league from Turin. I went thither yeſterday, and had the honour of waiting on the Queen, being preſented to her by her firſt lady of honour. I found her majeſty in a magnificent apartment, with a train of handſome ladies, all dreſſed in gowns, amongſt which it was eaſy to diſtinguiſh the fair Princeſs of Carignan. The Queen entertained me with a world of ſweetneſs and affability, and ſeemed miſtreſs of a great ſhare of good ſenſe. She did not forget to put me in mind of her Engliſh blood; and added, that ſhe always felt in herself a particular inclination to love the English. I returned her civility, by giving her the title of Majesty, as often as I could, which, perhaps, she will not have the comfort of hearing many months longer.—The King has a great deal of vivacity in his eyes; and the young Prince of Piedmont is a very handsome young man; but the great devotion which this court is, at present, fallen into, does not permit any of those entertainments proper for his age. Processions and masses are all the magnificence in fashion here; and gallantry is so criminal, that the poor Count of— who was our acquaintance at London, is very seriously disgraced, for some small overtures he presumed to make to a maid of honour. I intend to set out to morrow, and to pass those dreadful Alps, so much talked of.—If I come to the bottom you shall hear of me.—I am, etc. etc.

LETTER XLVII.

To Mrs. T——.

Lyons, *Sept.* 25. 1718.

I RECEIVED, at my arrival here, both your obliging letters, and also letters from many of my other friends, designed to Constantinople, and sent me from Marseilles hither; our merchant there, knowing we were upon our return. I am surprised to hear my sister—has left England. I suppose what I wrote to her from Turin will be lost, and where to direct I know not, having no account of her affairs from her own hand. For my own part, I am confined to my chamber, having kept my bed till yesterday, ever since the 17th, that I came to this town, where I have had so terrible a fever, I believed, for some time, that all my journies were ended here; and I do not at all wonder, that such fatigues as I have passed, should have such an effect. The first day's journey from Turin to Novalese, is through a very fine country, beautifully planted, and enriched by art and nature. The next day we began to ascend mount Cenis, being carried in little seats of twisted osiers, fixed upon poles, upon mens shoulders; our chaises taken to pieces, and laid upon mules.

The prodigious prospect of mountains covered with eternal snow, of clouds hanging far below our feet, and of vast cascades tumbling down the rocks with a confused roaring, would have been entertaining to me, if I had suffered less from the extreme cold that reigns here. But the misty rains which fall perpetually, penetrated even the thick fur I was wrapped in; and I was half dead with cold, before we got to the foot of the mountain, which was not till two hours after dark. This hill has a spacious plain on the top of it, and a fine lake there; but the descent is so steep and slippery, 'tis surprising to see these chairmen go so steadily as they do. Yet I was not half so much afraid of breaking my neck, as I was of falling sick; and the event has shewed, that I placed my fears right.

The other mountains are now all passable for a chaise, and very fruitful in vines and pastures. Amongst them is a breed of the finest goats in the world. Acquebellet is the last, and soon after we entered Pont Beauvoisin, the frontier town of France, whose bridge parts this kingdom, and the dominions of Savoy. The same night we arrived late at this town, where I have had nothing to do, but to take care of my health. I think myself already out of any danger, and am determined that the sore throat, which still remains, shall not confine me long. I am impatient to see the curiosities of this famous city, and more impatient to continue my journey to Paris, from whence I hope to write you a more diverting letter than 'tis possible for me to do now, with a mind weakened by sickness, a head muddled with spleen, from a sorry inn, and a chamber crammed with mortifying objects of apothecaries, vials and bottles.—I am, etc. etc.

LETTER XLVIII.

To Mr. Pope.

Lyons, Sept. 28. 1718.

I RECEIVED yours here, and should thank you for the pleasure you seem to enjoy from my return; but I can hardly forbear being angry at you, for rejoicing at what displeases me so much. You will think this but an odd compliment on my side. I'll assure you, 'tis not from insensibility of the joy of seeing my friends; but when I consider, that I must, at the same time, see and hear a thousand disagreeable impertinences; that I must receive and pay visits, make courtesies, and assist at tea-tables, where I shall be half killed with questions; and, on the other part, that I am a creature that cannot serve any body, but with insignificant good wishes; and that my presence is not a necessary good to any one member of my native country, I think I might much better have staid where ease and quiet made up the happiness of my indolent life.—I should certainly be melancholy, if I pursued this theme one line farther. I will rather fill the remainder of this paper with the inscriptions on the tables of brass, that are placed on each side of the town-house.

I. TABLE.

Maererum. nostr: : : : : si i : : : :
Equidem. primam. omnium. illam. cogitationem. hominum. quam. maxime. primam. occursuram. mihi. provideo.

deprecbr. ne. quaſt. novam. iſtam. rem. introduci. exhorreſcatis. ſed. illa. potius. cogitetis. quam. multa. in. hac. civitate. novata. ſint. et. quidem. ſtatim. ab. origine. urbis. noſtrae. in. quot. formas. ſtatuſque. res. p. noſtra. diducta. ſit.

Quondam. reges. hanc. tenuere. urbem. ne. tamen. domeſticis. ſucceſſoribus. eam. tradere. contigit. ſupervenere. alieni. et. quidam. externi. ut. Numa. Romulo. ſucceſſerit. ex. Sabinis. veniens. vicinus. quidem. ſed. tunc. externus. ut. Anco. Marcio. Priſcus. Tarquinius. propter. temeratum. ſanguinem. quod. patre. Demarato. Corinthio. natus. erat. et. Tarquinienſi. matre. generoſa. ſed. inopi. ut. quae. tali. marito. neceſſe. habuerit. ſuccumbere. cum. domi. repelleretur. a. gerendis. honoribus. poſtquam. Romam. migravit. regnum. adeptus. eſt. huic. quoque. et. filio. nepotive. ejus. nam. et. hoc.

inter. auctores. difcrepat. incertus. Servius. Tullius. fi. noftros. fequimur. captiva. natus. Ocrefia. fi. tufcos. coeli. quondam. Vivennae. fodalis. fideliffimus. omnisque. ejus. cafus. comes. poftquam. varia. fortuna. exactus. cum. omnibus. reliquis. coeliani. exercitus. Etruria. exceffit. montem. Coelium. occupavit. et. a. duce. fuo. Coelio. ita. appellitatus. mutatoque. nomine nam. tufce. Maftarna. ei. nomen. erat. ita. appellatus. eft. ut. dixi. et. regnum. fumma. cum. reip. utilitate. obtinuit. deinde. poftquam. Tarquini. Superbi. mores. invifi. civitati. noftrae. effe. coeperunt. qua. ipfius. qua. filiorum. ejus. nempe. pertaefum. eft. mentes. regni. et. ad. confules. annuos. magiftratus. adminiftratio. tranflata. eft.

Quid. nunc. commemorem. dictaturae. hoc. ipfo. confulari. imperium. valentius. repertum. apud. majores. noftros. quo. in. afperioribus. bellis. aut.

in. civili. motu. difficiliori. uterentur.
aut. in. auxilium. plebis. creatos. tri-
bunos. plebei. quid. a. confulibus. ad.
decemviros. tranflatum. imperium. fo-
lutoque. poftea. decemvirali. regno. ad.
confules. rurfus. reditum. quid. im : : :
v. ris. diftributum. confulare. imperium. tribunofque. militum. confulari.
imperio. appellatus. qui. feni. et. octo-
ni. crearentur. quid. communicatos. po-
ftremo. cum. plebe. honores. non. imperi. folum. fed. facerdotorum. quoque.
jamfi. narrem. bella. a. quibus. coepe-
rint. majores. noftri. et quo. proceffe-
rimus. vereor. ne. nimio. infolentior.
effe. videar. et. quaefiffe. jactationem.
gloriae. prolati. imperi. ultra. ocea-
num. fed. illo. C. Porius. revertar. ci-
vitatem.

II. TABLE.

: : : : : : : : : : : : : *fane* : : : :
: : : : : : : : : : : *novo* : : : *divus* :

aug : : : no : . : lus. et. patruus. Ti. Caefar. omnem. florem. ubique. coloniarum. ac. municipiorum. bonorum. fcilicet. virorum. et. locupletium. in. hac. curia. effe. voluit. quid. ergo. non. italicus. fenator. provinciali. potior. eft. jam. vobis. cum. hanc. partem. cenfurae. meae. approbare. caepero. quid de. ea. re. fentiam. rebus. oftendam. fed. ne. provinciales. quidem. fi. modo. ornare. curiam. poterint. rejiciendos. puto.

Ornatiffima. ecce. colonia. valentiffimaque. Riennenfium. quam. longo. jam. tempore. fenatores. huic. curiae. confert. ex. qua. colonia. inter. paucos. equeftris. ordinis. ornamentum. L. reftinum. familiariffime. diligo. et. hodieque. in. rebus. meis. detineo. cujus. liberi. fruantur. quaefo. primo. facerdotiorum. gradu. poft. modo. cum. annis. promoturi. dignitatis. fuae. incrementa. ut. dirum. nomen. latronis. taceam.

et. odi. illud. palestricum. prodiguum.
quod. ante. in. domum. consulatum.
intulit. quam. colonia. sua. solidum. ci-
vitatis. Romanae. beneficium. conse-
cuta. est. idem. de. fratre. ejus. possum.
dicere. miserabili. quidem. indignissi-
moque. hoc. casu. ut. vobis. utilis. se-
nator. esse. non. possit.

Tempus. est. jam. Ti. Caesar. Ger-
manice. detegere. te. patribus. conscrip-
tis. quo. tendat. oratio. tua. jam. enim.
ad. extremos. fines. Galliae. Narbonensis. venisti.

Tot. ecce. insignes. juvenes. quot. in-
tueor. non. magis. sunt. poenitendi.
senatorib. quam. poenitet. Persicum.
nobilissimum. virum. amicum. meum.
inter. imagines. majorum. suorum. Al-
lorogici. nomen. legere. quod. si. haec.
ita. esse. consenti. is. quid. ultra. de-
sideratis. quam. ut. vobis. digito. de-
monstrem. solum. ipsum. ultra. fines.
provinciae. Narbonensis. jam. vobis. se-

*natores. mittere. quando. ex. Lugduno.
habere. nos. noftri. ordinis. viros. non.
poenitet. timide. quidem. p. c. egreffus.
adfuetos. familiaresque. vobis. provinciarum. terminos. fum. fed. deftricte.
jam. comatae. Galliae. caufa. agenda.
eft. in. qua. fi. quis. hoc. intuetur. quod.
bello. per. decem. annos. exercuerunt.
divom. Julium. idem. opponat. centum.
annorum. immobilem. fidem. obfequiumque. multis. tripidis. rebus. noftris.
plufquam. expertum. illi. patri. meo.
Drufo. Germaniam. fubigenti. tutam.
quiete fua. fecuramque. a. tergo. pacem. praeftiterunt. et. quidem. cum. ad.
cenfus. novo. tum. opere. et. in. adfueto. Galliis. ad. bellum. avocatus. effet.
quod. opus. quam. arduum. fit. nobis.
nunc. cum.. maxime. quamvis. nihil.
ultra. quam. ut. publice. notae fint.
facultates. noftrae. exquiratur. nimis.
magno. experimento. cognofcimus.*

I was also shewed without the gate of St. Justinus, some remains of a Roman aqueduct; and behind the monastery of St. Mary, there are the ruins of the Imperial palace, where the Emperor Claudius was born, and where Severus lived. The great cathedral of St. John is a good Gothic building, and its clock much admired by the Germans. In one of the most conspicuous parts of the town, is the late King's statue set up, trampling upon mankind. I cannot forbear saying one word here, of the French statues (for I never intend to mention any more of them) with their gidded full bottomed wigs. If their King had intended to express, in one image, *ignorance*, *ill taste*, and *vanity*, his sculptors could have made no other figure, so proper for that purpose, as this statue, which represents the odd mixture of an old *beau*, who had a mind to be a hero, with a bushel of curled hair on his head and a gilt truncheon in his hand.—The French have been so voluminous on the history of this town, I need say nothing of it. The houses are tolerably well built, and the Belle Cour well planted, from whence is seen the celebrated joining of the Saone and Rhone.

„ Ubi Rhodanus ingens amne praerapido
fluit
„ Ararque dubitans quo suos fluctus agat."

I have had time to see every thing with great leisure, having been confined several days to this town by a swelling in my throat, the remains of a fever, occasioned by a cold I got in the damps of the Alps. The doctors here threaten me with all sorts of distempers, if I dare to leave them; but I, that know the obstinacy of it, think it just as possible to continue my way to Paris, with it, as to go about the streets of Lyons; and am determined to pursue my journey to-morrow, in spite of doctors, apothecaries, and sore throats.

When you see Lady R—, tell her I have received her letter, and will answer it from Paris, believing that the place that she would most willingly hear of.

I am, etc. etc.

LETTER XLIX.

To the Lady R——.

Paris, Oct. 10. 1718.

I CANNOT give my dear Lady R—— a better proof of the pleasure I have in writing to her, than chusing to do it in this seat of various amusements, where I am *accablée* with visits, and those so full of vivacity and compliments, that 'tis full employment enough to hearken; whether one answers or not. The French Ambassadress at Constantinople, has a very considerable and numerous family, here, who all come to see me, and are never weary of making inquiries. The air of Paris has already had a good effect on me; for I was never in better health; though I have been extremely ill all the road from Lyons to this place. You may judge how agreeable the journey has been to me; which did not want that addition to make me dislike it. I think nothing so terrible as objects of misery, except one had the Godlike attribute of being capable to redress them; and all the country villages of France shew nothing else. While the post horses are changed, the whole town comes out to beg, with such miserable starved faces, and thin tattered clothes, they need no other eloquence, to persuade one of the wretchedness of their condition. This is all the French magnificence, till you come to Fontainebleau, where you are shewed one thousand five hundred rooms in the King's hunting palace. The apartments of the royal family are very large, and richly gilt; but I saw nothing in the architecture or painting worth remembering. The long gallery, built by Henry IV. has prospects of all the King's houses. Its walls are designed after the taste of those times, but appear now very mean. The park is, indeed, finely wooded and watered, the trees well grown and planted, and in the fish-ponds are kept tame carps, said to be, some of them, eighty years of age. The late King passed some months every year at this seat; and all the rocks round it, by the pious sentences inscribed on them, shew the devotion in fashion at his court, which I believe died with him; at least, I see no exterior marks of it at Paris, where all people's thoughts seem to be on present diversion.

The fair of St. Laurence is now in season. You may be sure I have been carried thither, and think it much better disposed than ours of Bartholomew. The shops being all set in rows so regularly and well lighted, they made up a very agreeable spectacle. But I was not at all satisfied with the *grossierté* of their harlequin, no more than with their music at the opera, which was abominably grating, after being used to that of Italy. Their house is a booth, compared to that of the Hay-market, and the play-house not so neat as that of Lincoln's-Inn-fields; but then it must be owned, to their praise, their tragedians are much beyond any of ours. I should hardly allow Mrs. O——d a better place than to be confidante to La——. I have seen the tragedy of Bajazet so well represented, that I think our best actors can be only said to speak, but these to feel; and it is certainly infinitely more moving to see a man appear unhappy, than to hear him say that he is so, with a jolly face, and a stupid smirk in his countenance.—*A propos* of countenances, I must tell you something of the French ladies; I have seen all the beauties, and such— —(I can't help making use of the coarse word) nauseous creatures! so fantastically absurd in their dress! so monstrously unnatural in their paints! their hair cut short, and curled round their faces, and so loaded with powder, that it makes it look like white wool! and on their cheeks to their chins, unmercifully laid on a shining red japan, that glistens in a most flaming manner, so that they seem to have no resemblance to human faces. I am apt to believe, that they took the first hint of their dress from a fair sheep newly ruddled. It is with pleasure I recollect my dear pretty country-women; and writing to any body else, I should say, that these grotesque daubers give me still a higher esteem of the natural charms of dear Lady R— —'s auburne hair, and the lively colours of her unsullied complexion.

I am, etc. etc.

P. S. I have met the Abbé here, who defires me to make his compliments to you.

LETTER L.

To Mr. T——.

Paris, Oct. 16. 1718.

YOU fee I am juft to my word, in writing to you from Paris, where I was very much furprifed to meet my fifter; I need not add, very much pleafed. She as little expected to fee me as I her (having not received my late letters;) and this meeting would fhine under the hand of de Scuderie; but I fhall not imitate his ftyle fo far, as to tell you how often we embraced, how fhe inquired, by what odd chance I returned from Conftantinople? And I anfwered her by afking, what adventure brought her to Paris? To fhorten the ftory, all queftions, and answers, and exclamations, and compliments being over, we agreed upon running about together, and have seen Versailles, Trianon, Marli, and St. Cloud. We had an order for the water to play for our diversion, and I was followed thither, by all the English at Paris. I own, Versailles appeared to me rather vast than beautiful; and after having seen the exact proportions of the Italian buildings, I thought the irregularity of it shocking.

The King's cabinet of antiques and medals, is, indeed, very richly furnished. Amongst that collection, none pleased so well, as the apotheosis of Germanicus, on a large agate, which is one of the most delicate pieces of the kind that I remember to have seen. I observed some ancient statues of great value. But the nauseous flattery, and tawdry pencil of Le Brun, are equally disgusting in the gallery. I will not pretend to describe to you the great apartment, the vaſt variety of fountains, the theatre, the grove of Aeſop's fables etc. all which you may read very amply particularized in ſome of the French authors, that have been paid for theſe deſcriptions. Trianon, in its littleneſs, pleaſed me better than Verſailles; Marli, better than either of them; and St. Cloud beſt of all, having the advantage of the Seine running at the bottom of the gardens, the great caſcade, etc. You may find information in the aforeſaid books, if you have any curioſity to know the exact number of the ſtatues, and how many feet they caſt up the water.

We ſaw the King's pictures in the magnificent houſe of the Duke D' Antin, who has the care of preſerving them till his Majeſty is of age. There are not many, but of the beſt hands. I looked with great pleaſure on the Archangel of Raphael, where the ſentiments of ſuperior beings are as well expreſſed as in Milton. You won't forgive me, if I ſay nothing of the Thuilleries, much finer than our Mall; and the Cour, more agreeable than our Hide-Park, the high trees giving ſhade in the hotteſt ſeaſon. At the Louvre, I had the opportunity of ſeeing the King, accompanied by the Duke Regent. He is tall, and well ſhaped, but has not the air of holding the crown ſo many years as his great grandfather. And now I am ſpeaking of the court, I muſt ſay, I ſaw nothing in France, that delighted me ſo much, as to ſee an Engliſhman (at leaſt a Briton) abſolute at Paris; I mean Mr. Law, who treats their Dukes and Peers, extremely *de haut en bas*, and is treated by them with the utmoſt ſubmiſſion and reſpect.—Poor ſouls!— —This reflection on their abject ſlavery, puts me in mind of the *place des victoires;* but I will not take up your time, and my own, with such descriptions, which are too numerous.

In general, I think Paris has the advantage of London, in the neat pavement of the streets, and the regular lighting of them at nights, in the proportion of the streets, the houses being all built of stone, and most of those belonging to people of quality, being beautified by gardens. But we certainly may boast of a town very near twice as large; and when I have said that, I know nothing else we surpass it in. I shall not continue here long; if you have any thing to command me during my short stay, write soon, and I shall take pleasure in obeying you,

I am, etc. etc.

LETTER LI.

To the Abbot —— ——.

Dover, Oct. 31. 1718.

I AM willing to take your word for it, that I shall really oblige you, by letting you know, as soon as possible, my safe passage over the water. I arrived this morning at Dover, after being tossed a whole night in the packet-boat, in so violent a manner, that the master, considering the weakness of his vessel, thought it proper to remove the mail, and gave us notice of the danger. We called a little fishing-boat, which could hardly make up to us; while all the people on board us were crying to heaven. 'Tis hard to imagine one's self in a scene of greater horrour than on such an occasion: and yet, shall I own it to you? though I was not at all willing to be drowned, I could not forbear being entertained at the double

distress of a fellow-passenger. She was an English lady that I had met at Calais, who desired me to let her go over with me in my cabin. She had bought a fine point-head, which she was contriving to conceal from the custom-house officers. When the wind grew high, and our little vessel cracked, she fell very heartily to her prayers, and thought wholly of her soul. When it seemed to abate, she returned to the worldly care of her head-dress, and adressed herself to me——
„ *Dear Madam, will you take care of*
„ *this point? if it should be lost!*——
„ *Ah, Lord, we shall all be lost!*—
„—*Lord have mercy on my soul!*—
„—*Pray, Madam, take care of this*
„ *head-dress.*" This easy transition from her soul to her head-dress, and the alternate agonies that both gave her, made it hard to determine which she thought of greatest value. But, however, the scene was not so diverting, but I was glad to

get rid of it, and be thrown into the little boat, though with some hazard of breaking my neck. It brought me safe hither; and I cannot help looking with partial eyes on my native land. That partiality was certainly given us by nature, to prevent rambling, the effect of an ambitious thirst after knowledge, which we are not formed to enjoy. All we get by it, is a fruitless desire of mixing the different pleasures and conveniences which are given to the different parts of the world, and cannot meet in any one of them. After having read all that is to be found in the languages I am mistress of, and having decayed my sight by midnight studies, I envy the easy peace of mind of a ruddy milk-maid, who undisturbed by doubt, hears the sermon, with humility, every Sunday, not having confounded the sentiments of natural duty in her head by the vain inquiries of the schools, who may be more learned, yet, after all, muſt remain as ignorant. And, after having ſeen part of Aſia and Africa, and almoſt made the tour of Europe, I think the honeſt Engliſh ſquire more happy, who verily believes the Greek wines leſs delicious than March beer; that the African fruits have not ſo fine a flavour as golden pippins; that the Beca figuas of Italy are not ſo well taſted as a rump of beef; and that, in ſhort, there is no perfect enjoyment of this life out of Old England. I pray God I may think ſo for the reſt of my life; and, ſince I muſt be contented with our ſcanty allowance of daylight, that I may forget the enlivening ſun of Conſtantinople.

I am, etc. etc.

LETTER LII.

To Mr. Pope.

Dover, Nov. 1. 1718.

I HAVE this minute received a letter of yours, sent me from Paris. I believe and hope I shall very soon see both you and Mr. Congreve; but as I am here in an inn, where we stay to regulate our march to London, bag and baggage, I shall employ some of my leisure time, in answering that part of yours, that seems to require an answer.

I must applaud your good nature, in supposing, that your pastoral lovers (vulgarly called hay-makers) would have lived in everlasting joy and harmony, if the lightning had not interrupted their scheme of happiness. I see no reason to imagine, that John Hughes and Sarah Drew, were either wiser or more virtuous than their neighbours. That a well-set man of twenty-five, should have a fancy to marry a brown woman of eighteen, is nothing marvellous; and I cannot help thinking, that had they married, their lives would have passed in the common track with their fellow parishioners. His endeavouring to shield her from a storm, was a natural action, and what he would have certainly done for his horse, if he had been in the same situation. Neither am I of opinion, that their sudden death was a reward of their mutual virtue. You know the Jews were reproved for thinking a village destroyed by fire, more wicked than those that had escaped the thunder. Time and chance happen to all men. Since you desire me to try my skill in an epitaph, I think the following lines perhaps more just, tho' not so poetical as yours.

Here lies John Hughes and Sarah Drew;
Perhaps you'll say, What's that to you?

Believe me, friend, much may be said
On that poor couple that are dead.
On Sunday next they should have married:
But see how oddly things are carried!
On Thursday last it rain'd and lighten'd,
These tender lovers sadly frighten'd,
Shelter'd beneath the cocking hay,
In hopes to pass the time away.
But the bold thunder found them out,
(Commissioned for that end no doubt)
And seizing on their trembling breath,
Consign'd them to the shades of death.
Who knows if 'twas not kindly done?
For had they seen the next year's sun,
A beaten wife and cuckold swain
Had jointly curs'd the marriage chain:
Now they are happy in their doom,
For Pope has wrote upon their tomb.

I confess, the sentiments are not altogether so heroic as yours; but I hope you will forgive them in favour of the two last lines. You see how much I esteem the honour you have done them; though I am not very impatient to have the same, and had rather continue to be your stupid, *living*, humble fervant, than be *celebrated* by all the pens in Europe.

I would write to Mr. Congreve; but fuppofe you will read this to him, if he inquires after me.

End of the Third Volume.

LETTERS

OF THE
RIGHT HONOURABLE
LADY MARY WORTLEY
MONTAGUE.

VOLUME IV.

LETTER LIII. *)

To Lady ——.

January 23. 1715-16.

I FIND, after all, by your letter of yesterday, that Mrs. D——is resolved to marry the old greasy curate. She was always high-church in an excessive degree; and, you know, she used to speak of Sacheverel as an apostolic Saint, who was worthy to sit in the same place with St. Paul, if not a step above him. It is a matter, however, very doubtful to me, whether it is not still more the *man* than the *apostle* that Mrs. D—— looks to in the present alliance. Though at the age of forty, she is, I assure you, very far from being cold and insensible;

*) This and the following letters are now first published.

her fire may be covered with afhes, but it is not extinguifhed.— —Don't be deceived, my dear, by that prudifh and fanctified air.— —Warm devotion is no equivocal mark of warm paffions; befides, I know it is a fact, (of which I have proofs in hand, which I will tell you by word of mouth) that our learned and holy prude is exceedingly difpofed to ufe the *means*, fuppofed in the primitive command, let what will come of the end. The curate indeed is very filthy.— — Such a red, fpungy, warty nofe! Such a fquint!— —In fhort, he is ugly beyond expreffion; and, what ought naturally to render him peculiarly difpleafing to one of Mrs. D—'—'s conftitution and propenfities, he is ftricken in years. Nor do I really know how they will live. He has but forty-five pounds a-year— — fhe but a trifling fum; fo that they are likely to feaft upon love and ecclefiaftical hiftory, which will be very empty food, without a proper mixture of beef and pudding. I have, however, engaged our friend, who is the curate's landlord, to give them a good leafe; and if Mrs. D——, inſtead of ſpending whole days in reading Collier, Hicks, and vile tranſlations of Plato and Epictetus, will but form the reſolution of taking care of her houſe, and minding her dairy, things may go tolerably. It is not likely that their *tender loves* will give them many *ſweet babes* to provide for.

I met the lover yeſterday, going to he ale-houſe in his dirty night-gown, twith a book under his arm, to entertain the club; and, as Mrs. D——was with me at the time, I pointed out to her the charming creature: ſhe bluſhed, and looked prim; but quoted a paſſage out of Herodotus, in which it is ſaid that the Perſians wore long night-gowns. There is really no more accounting for the taſte in marriage of many of our ſex, than there is for the appetite of your neighbour Mifs S—y, who makes fuch wafte of chalk and charcoal, when they fall in her way.

As marriage produces children, fo children produce care and difputes; and wrangling, as is faid (at leaft by old bachelors and old maids) is one of the *fweets* of the conjugal ftate. You tell me that our friend Mrs. ——is, at length, bleffed with a fon, and that her hufband, who is a great philofopher, (if his own teftimony is to be depended upon) infifts on her fuckling it herfelf. You afk my advice on this matter; and, to give it you frankly, I really think that Mr. ——'s demand is unreafonable, as his wife's conftitution is tender, and her temper fretful. A true philofopher would confider thefe circumftances; but a pedant is always throwing his fyftem in your face, and applies it equally to all things, times and places, juft like a tailor who would make a coat out of his own head, without any regard to the bulk or figure of the perſon that muſt wear it. All thoſe fine-ſpun arguments that he has drawn from nature, to ſtop your mouths, weigh, I muſt own to you, but very little with me. This ſame *Nature* is, indeed, a ſpecious word, nay there is a great deal in it, if it is properly underſtood and applied; but I cannot bear to hear people uſing it, to juſtify what common ſenſe muſt diſavow. Is not nature modified by art in many things? Was it not deſigned to be ſo? And is it not happy for human ſociety, that it is ſo? Would you like to ſee your huſband let his beard grow, until he would be obliged to put the end of it in his pocket, becauſe this beard is the gift of nature? The inſtincts of nature point out neither tailors, nor weavers, nor mantua-makers, nor ſemp- ſters, nor milliners; and yet I am very glad that we do not run naked like the

Hottentots. But not to wander from the subject—I grant that nature has furnished the mother with milk to nourish her child; but I maintain, at the same time, that if she can find better milk elsewhere, she ought to prefer it without hesitation. I don't see why she should have more scruple to do this, than her husband has to leave the clear fountain which nature gave him, to quench his thirst, for stout october, port, or claret. Indeed, if Mrs. ——was a buxom, sturdy woman, who lived on plain food, took regular exercise, enjoyed proper returns of rest, and was free from violent passions, (which you and I know is not the case) she might be a good nurse for her child; but, as matters stand, I do verily think, that the milk of a good comely cow, who feeds quietly in her meadow, never devours ragouts, nor drinks ratafia, nor frets at quadrille, nor sits up till three in the morning, elated with gain, or dejected with lofs; I do think, that the milk of fuch a cow, or of a nurfe that came as near it as poffible, would be likely to nourifh the young fquire much better than her's. If it be true that the child fucks in the mother's paffions with her milk, this is a ftrong argument in favour of the cow, unlefs you may be afraid that the young fquire may become a calf; but how many calves are there both in ftate and church, who have been brought up with their mother's milk?

I promife faithfully, to communicate to no mortal, the letter you wrote me laft.—What you fay of two of the rebel lords, I believe be true; but I can do nothing in the matter.—If my projects don't fail in the execution, I fhall fee you before a month paffes. Give my fervice to Dr. Blackbeard.—He is a good man, but I never faw in my life, fuch a perfecuting face cover a humane and tender heart. I imagine, within myfelf, that the Smithfield priests, who burned the protestants in the time of Queen Mary, had just such faces as the doctor's. If we were papists, I should like him very much for my confessor; his seeming austerity would give you and me a great reputation for sanctity; and his good, indulgent heart, would be the very thing that would suit us, in the affair of penance and ghostly direction.

Farewell, my dear Lady, etc. etc.

LETTER LIV.

To the Abbot —— ——.

Vienna, Jan. 2. 1717.

I AM really almost tired with the life of Vienna. I am not, indeed, an enemy to dissipation and hurry, much less to amusement and pleasure; but I cannot endure, long, even pleasure, when it is fettered with formality, and assumes the air of syſtem. 'Tis true I have had here ſome very agreeable connexions; and what will perhaps ſurpriſe you, I have particular pleaſure in my Spaniſh acquaintances, count Oropeſa and general Puebla. Theſe two noblemen are much in the good graces of the Emperor, and yet they ſeem to be brewing miſchief. The court of Madrid cannot reflect, without pain, upon the territories that were cut off from the Spaniſh monarchy by the peace of Utrecht, and it ſeems to be looking wiſhfully out, for an opportunity of getting them back again. That is a matter about which I trouble myſelf very little; let the court be in the right or in the wrong, I like mightily the two counts its ministers. I dined with them both ſome days ago at count Wurmbrand's, an aulic counſellor, and a man of letters, who is univerſally eſteemed here. But the firſt man at this court, in point of knowledge and abilities, is certainly count Schlick, high chancellor of Bohemia, whose immense reading is accompanied with a fine taste and a solid judgment; he is a declared enemy to prince Eugene, and a warm friend to the honest hot-headed marshal Staremberg. One of the most accomplished men I have seen at Vienna, is the young count Tarrocco, who accompanies the amiable prince of Portugal. I am almost in love with them both, and wonder to see such elegant manners, and such free and generous sentiments in two young men that have hitherto seen nothing but their own country. The count is just such a Roman-catholic as you; he succeeds greatly with the devout beauties here; his first overtures in gallantry are disguised under the luscious strains of spiritual love, that were sung formerly by the sublimely voluptuous Fenelon, and the tender Madam Guion, who turned the fire of carnal love to divine objects: thus the count begins with the *spirit*, and ends generally with the *flesh*, when he makes his addresses to holy virgins.

I made acquaintance yesterday with the famous poet Rousseau, who lives here under the peculiar protection of Prince Eugene, by whose liberality he subsists. He passes here for a free-thinker, and, what is still worse in my esteem, for a man whose heart does not feel the encomiums he gives to virtue and honour in his poems. I like his odes mightily! they are much superior to the lyric productions of our English poets, few of whom have made any figure in that kind of poetry. I don't find that learned men abound here; there is, indeed, a prodigious number of alchymists at Vienna; the *philosophers' stone* is the great object of zeal and science; and those who have more reading and capacity than the vulgar, have transfported their superstition (shall I call it?) or fanaticism, from religion to chymistry; and they believe in a new kind of transubstantiation, which is designed to make the laity as rich as the other kind has made the priesthood. This pestilential passion has already ruined several great houses. There is scarcely a man of opulence or fashion, that has not an alchymist in his service, and even the Emperor is supposed to be no enemy to this folly, in secret, though he has pretended to discourage it in public.

Prince Eugene was so polite as to shew me his library yesterday; we found him attended by Rousseau, and his favourite count, Bonneval, who is a man of wit, and is here thought to be a very bold and enterprizing spirit. The library, though not very ample, is well chosen; but as the prince will admit into it no editions but what are beautiful and pleasing to the eye, and there are, nevertheless, numbers of excellent books that are but indifferently printed, this finikin and foppish taste makes many disagreeable chasms in this collection. The books are pompously bound in Turkey leather; and two of the most famous bookbinders of Paris, were expressly sent for to do this work. Bonneval pleasantly told me, that there were several quarto's, on the art of war, that were bound with the skins of *Spahis* and *Janizaries*: and this jest, which was indeed elegant, raised a smile of pleasure on the grave countenance of the famous warriour. The prince, who is a connoisseur in the fine arts, shewed me, with particular pleasure, the famous collection of portraits that formerly belonged to Fouquet, and which he purchased at an excessive price. He has augmented it with a considerable number of new acquisitions; so that he has now in his possession such a collection in that kind, as you will scarcely find in any ten cabinets in Europe. If I told you the number, you will say that I make an indiscreet use of the permission to lie, which is more or less given to travellers, by the indulgence of the candid.

Count Tarrocco is just come in.—He is the only person I have excepted, this morning, in my general order to receive no company.—I think I see you smile;—but I am not so far gone as to stand in need of absolution; though, as the human heart is deceitful, and the count very agreeable, you may think, that even though I should not want an absolution, I would, nevertheless, be glad to have an indulgence.—No such thing.—However, as I am an heretic, and you no confessor, I shall make no declarations on this head.—The design of the count's visit is a ball;—more pleasure.—I shall be surfeited.

Adieu, etc.

LETTER LV.

To Mr. Pope.

Sept. 1. 1717.

WHEN I wrote to you laſt, Belgrade was in the hands of the Turks; but, at this preſent moment, it has changed maſters, and is in the hands of the Imperialiſts. A janizary, who, in nine days, and yet without any wings but what a panic terrour ſeems to have furniſhed, arrived at Conſtantinople from the army of the Turks before Belgrade, brought Mr. Wortley the news of a complete victory obtained by the Imperialiſts, commanded by prince Eugene, over the Ottoman troops. It is ſaid, the prince has diſcovered great conduct and valour in this action; and I am particularly glad that the voice of glory and duty has called him from the— —*(here ſeveral words of the manuſcript are effaced)*

—Two days after the battle, the town furrendered. The confternation, which this defeat has occafioned here, is inexpreffible; and the Sultan, apprehending a revolution, from the refentment and indignation of the people, fomented by certain leaders, has begun his precautions, after the goodly fafhion of this bleffed government, by ordering feveral perfons to be ftrangled, who were the objects of his royal fufpicion. He has alfo ordered his treafurer to advance fome months pay to the janizaries, which feems the lefs neceffary, as their conduct has been bad in this campaign, and their licentious ferocity feems pretty well tamed by the public contempt. Such of them as return in ftraggling and fugitive parties to the metropolis, have not fpirit nor credit enough to defend themfelves from the infults of the mob; the very children taunt them, and the populace fpit in their faces as they pafs. They

refused, during the battle, to lend their
affiftance to fave the baggage and military cheft, which, however, were defended by the Bafhaws and their retinue,
while the janizaries and fpahis were nobly
employed in plundering their own camp.

You fee here, that I give you a very
handfome return for your obliging letter.
You entertain me with a moft agreeable
account of your amiable connexions with
men of letters and tafte, and of the delicious moments you pafs in their fociety
under the rural fhade; and I exhibit to
you, in return, the barbarous fpectacle
of Turks and Germans cutting one another's throats. But what can you expect
from fuch a country as this, from which the
mufes have fled, from which letters feem
eternally banifhed, and in which you
fee, in private fcenes, nothing purfued
as happinefs, but the refinements of an
indolent voluptuoufnefs, and where thofe
who act upon the public theatre live in

uncertainty, fufpicion, and terrour? Here, pleafure, to which I am no enemy, when it is properly feafoned, and of a good compofition, is furely of the cloying kind Veins of wit, elegant converfation, eafy commerce, are unknown among the Turks; and yet they feem capable of all thefe, if the vile fpirit of their government did not ftifle genius, damp curiofity, and fupprefs an hundred paffions, that embellifh and render live agreeable. The lufcious paffion of the feraglio, is the only one almoft that is gratified here to the full; but it is blended fo with the furly fpirit of defpotifm in one of the parties, and with the dejection and anxiety which this fpirit produces in the other, that, to one of my way of thinking, it cannot appear otherwife than as a very mixed kind of enjoyment. The women here are not, indeed, fo clofely confined as many have related; they enjoy a high degree of liberty, even in the bosom of servitude; and they have methods of evasion and disguise, that are very favourable to gallantry; but, after all, they are still under uneasy apprehensions of being discovered; and a discovery exposes them to the most merciless rage of jealousy, which is here a monster that cannot be satiated but with blood. The magnificence and riches that reign in the apartments of the ladies of fashion here, seem to be one of their chief pleasures, joined with their retinue of female slaves, whose music, dancing, and dress, amuse them highly; but there is such an air of form and stiffness amidst this grandeur, as hinders it from pleasing me at long-run, however I was dazzled with it at first sight. This stiffness and formality of manners, are peculiar to the Turkish ladies; for the Grecian belles are of quite another character and complexion; with them, pleasure appears in more engaging forms, and their persons, manners, conversations and amusements, are very far from being destitute of elegance and ease.—

I received the news of Mr. Addison's being declared secretary of state with the less surprise, in that I know that post was almost offered to him before. At that time he declined it; and I really believe, that he would have done well to have declined it now. Such a post as that, and such a wife as the Countess, do not seem to be, in prudence, eligible for a man that is asthmatic; and we may see the day, when he will be heartily glad to resign them both. It is well that he laid aside the thoughts of the voluminous dictionary, of which I have heard you or somebody else frequently make mention. But no more on that subject; I would not have said so much, were I not assured, that this letter will come safe and unopened to hand. I long much to tread upon English ground, that I may see you and Mr. Congreve, who render that ground *claſſic ground;* nor will you refuſe our preſent ſecretary a part of that merit, whatever reaſons you may have to be diſſatisfied with him in other reſpects. You are the three happieſt poets I ever heard of; one a ſecretary of ſtate, the other enjoying leiſure, with dignity, in two lucrative employments, and you, though your religious profeſſion is an obſtacle to court promotion, and diſqualifies you from filling civil employments, have found the *philoſophers' ſtone;* ſince, by making the Iliad paſs through your poetical crucible into an Engliſh form, without loſing aught of its original beauty, you have drawn the golden current of Pactolus to Twickenham. I call this finding the philoſophers' ſtone, ſince you alone found out the ſecret, and nobody elſe has got into it. Addiſon and Tickel tried it, but their experiments failed; and they loſt, if not their money, at least a certain portion of their fame in the trial——while you touched the mantle of the divine bard, and imbibed his spirit. I hope we shall have the Odyssey soon from your happy hand; and I think I shall follow with singular pleasure, the traveller Ulysses, who was an observer of men and manners, when he travels in your harmonious numbers. I love him much better than the hot-headed son of Peleus, who bullied his general, cried for his mistress, and so on. It is true, the excellence of the Iliad does not depend upon his merit or dignity; but I wish, nevertheless, that Homer had chosen a hero somewhat less pettish and less fantastic: a perfect hero is chimerical and unnatural, and consequently uninstructive; but it is also true, that while the epic hero ought to be drawn with the infirmities that are the lot of humanity, he ought never to be represented as extremely absurd. But

it becomes me ill to play the critic; fo
I take my leave of you for this time,
and defire you will believe me, with
the higheſt eſteem,

      Yours, etc.

LETTER LVI. *)

To the Countess of ——

Saturday— —Florence.

I SET out from Bologna the moment
I had finiſhed the letter I wrote you on
Monday laſt, and ſhall now continue to
inform you of the things that have ſtruck
me moſt in this excurſion. Sad roads—,
—hilly and rocky— —between Bologna

*) As this letter is the fupplement to a
preceeding one, which is not come to the
hands of the editor, it was probably, on
that account, fent without a date. It feems
evidently to have been written after Lady
M. W. M. had fixed her refidence in Italy.

and Firenzuola. Between this latter place and Florence, I went out of my road to visit the monastery of *La Trappe*, which is of French origin, and one of the most austere and self-denying orders I have met with. In this gloomy retreat, it gave me pain to observe the infatuation of men, who have devoutly reduced themselves to a much worse condition than that of the beasts. Folly, you see, is the lot of humanity, whether it arises in the flowery paths of pleasure, or the thorny ones of an ill-judged devotion. But of the two sorts of fools, I shall always think that the merry one has the most eligible fate; and I cannot well form a notion of that spiritual and extatic joy, that is mixed with sighs, groans, hunger and thirst, and the other complicated miseries of monastic discipline. It is a strange way of going to work for happiness, to excite an enmity between soul and body, which nature and providence have designed to live together in an union and friendship, and which we cannot separate like man and wife, when they happen to disagree. The profound silence that is enjoined upon the monks of *La Trappe*, is a singular circumstance of their unsociable and unnatural discipline, and were this injunction never to be dispensed with, it would be needless to visit them in any other character than as a collection of statues; but the superior of the convent suspended, in our favour, that rigorous law, and allowed one of the mutes to converse with me, and answer a few discreet questions. He told me, that the monks of this order in France, are still more austere than those of Italy, as they never taste wine, flesh, fish, or eggs; but live entirely upon vegetables. The story that is told of the institution of this order, is remarkable, and is well attested, if my information be good. Its founder was a French Nobleman, whose name was Bouthillier de Rancé, a man of pleasure and gallantry, which were converted into the deepest gloom of devotion by the following incident. His affairs obliged him to absent himself, for some time, from a lady with whom he had lived in the most intimate and tender connexions of successful love. At his return to Paris, he proposed to surprise her agreeably, and, at the same time, to satisfy his own impatient desire of seeing her, by going directly, and without ceremony, to her apartment by a back-stair, which he was well acquainted with.—But think of the spectacle that presented itself to him at his entrance into the chamber that had so often been the scene of love's highest raptures! his mistress dead—dead of the small-pox— —disfigured beyond expression— —a loathsome mass of putrified matter—and the surgeon separating the head from the body, because the coffin had been made too short! He stood for a moment motionless in amazement, and filled with horrour—and then retired from the world, shut himself up in the convent of *La Trappe*, where he passed the remainder of his days in the most cruel and disconsolate devotion.—Let us quit this sad subject.

I must not forget to tell you, that before I came to this monastery, I went to see the burning mountains near Firenzuola, of which the naturalists speak as a great curiosity. The flame it sends forth is without smoke, and resembles brandy set on fire. The ground about it is well cultivated, and the fire appears only in one spot where there is a cavity, whose circumference is small, but in it are several crevices, whose depths are unknown. It is remarkable, that when a piece of wood is thrown into this cavity, though it cannot pass through the crevices, yet it is consumed in a moment;

and that though the ground about it be perfectly cold, yet if a ſtick be rubbed with any force againſt it, it emits a flame, which, however, is neither hot nor durable like that of the volcano. If you defire a more circumſtantial account of this phenomenon, and have made a ſufficient progreſs in Italian, to read father Carazzi's defcription of it, you need not be at a loſs, for I have ſent this defcription to Mr. F——, and you have only to aſk it of him. After obſerving the volcano, I ſcrambled up all the neighbouring hills, partly on horſeback, partly on foot, but could find no veſtige of fire in any of them; though common report would make one believe that they all contain volcano's.

 I hope you have not taken it in your head to expect from me a defcription of the famous gallery here, where I arrived on Thurſday at noon; this would be requiring a volume inſtead of a letter;

besides I have as yet seen but a part of this immense treasure, and I propose employing some weeks more to survey the whole. You cannot imagine any situation more agreeable than Florence. It lies in a fertile and smiling valley watered by the Arno, which runs through the city; and nothing can surpass the beauty and magnificence of its public buildings, particularly the cathedral, whose grandeur filled me with astonishment. The palaces, squares, fountains, statues, bridges, do not only carry an aspect full of elegance and greatness, but discover a taste quite different in kind, from that which reigns in the public edifices in other countries. The more I see of Italy, the more I am persuaded that the Italians have a style (if I may use that expression) in every thing, which distinguished them almost essentially from all other Europeans. Where they have got it,———whether from natural genius or ancient imitation and inheritance, I shall not examine; but the fact is certain. I have been but one day in the gallery, that amazing repository of the most precious remains of antiquity, and which alone is sufficient to immortalize the illustrious house of Medicis, by whom it was built, and enriched as we now see it. I was so impatient to see the famous Venus of Medicis, that I went hastily through six apartments, in order to get a sight of this divine figure, purposing, when I had satisfied this ardent curiosity, to return and view the rest at my leisure. As I, indeed, passed through the great room which contains the ancient statues, I was stopped short at viewing the Antinous, which they have placed near that of Adrian, to revive the remembrance of their preposterous loves; which I suppose, the Florentines rather look upon as an object of envy, than of horrour and disgust. This statue, like that of the

Venus de Medicis, spurns description; such figures my eyes never beheld.—I can now understand that Ovid's comparing a fine woman to a statue, which I formerly thought a very disobliging similitude, was the nicest and highest piece of flattery. The Antinous is entirely naked, all its parts are bigger than nature; but the whole, taken together, and the fine attitude of the figure, carry such an expression of ease, elegance, and grace, as no words can describe. When I saw the Venus, I was rapt in wonder, —and I could not help casting a thought back upon Antinous. They ought to be placed together; they are worthy of each other.—If marble could see and feel, the separation might be prudent,—if it could only *see*, it would certainly lose its coldness, and learn to feel, and, in such a case, the charms of these two figures would produce an effect quite opposite to that of the Gorgon's head, which turned flesh into stone. Did I pretend to describe to you the Venus, it would only set your imagination at work to form ideas of her figure; and your ideas would no more resemble that figure, than the Portuguese face of Miss N— —, who has enchanted our knights, resembles the sweet and graceful countenance of lady— —, his former flame. The description of a face or figure, is a needless thing, as it never conveys a true idea; it only gratifies the imagination with a fantastic one, until the real one is seen. So, my dear, if you have a mind to form a true notion of the divine forms and features of the Venus and Antinous, come to Florence.

I would be glad to oblige you and your friend Vertue, by executing your commission with respect to the sketches of Raphael's cartoons at Hampton-court; but I cannot do it to my satisfaction. I have, indeed, seen, in the Grand Duke's collection, four pieces, in which that wonderful artist had thrown freely from his pencil the first thoughts and rude lines of some of these compositions; and as the first thoughts of a great genius are precious, these pieces attracted my curiosity in a particular manner; but when I went to examine them closely, I found them so damaged and effaced, that they did not at all answer my expectation. Whether this be owing to negligence or envy, I cannot say; I mention the latter, because it is notorious, that many of the modern painters have discovered ignoble marks of envy at a view of the inimitable productions of the ancients. Instead of employing their art to preserve the master-pieces of antiquity, they have endeavoured to destroy and efface many of them. I have seen with my own eyes an evident proof of this at Bologna, where the greatest part of the paintings in fresco on the walls of the convent of St. Michael in Bosco, done by the Carracci, and Guido Rheni, have been ruined by the painters, who, after having copied some of the finest heads, scraped them almost entirely out with nails. Thus, you see, nothing is exempt from human malignity.

The word malignity, and a passage in your letter, call to my mind the wicked wasp of Twickenham; his lies affect me now no more; they will be all as much despised as the story of the seraglio and the handkerchief, of which I am persuaded he was the only inventor. That man has a malignant and ungenerous heart; and he is base enough to assume the mask of a moralist, in order to decry human nature, and to give a decent vent to his hatred to man and woman kind.—But I must quit this contemptible subject, on which a just indignation would render my pen so fertile, that after having fatigued you with a long letter, I would surfeit you with a supplement twice as long. Besides, a violent head-ach advertises me that it is time to lay down my pen and get me to bed. I shall say some things to you in my next, that I would have you to impart to the *strange man*, as from yourself. My mind is at present tolerably quiet: if it were as dead to sin, as it is to certain connexions, I should be a great Saint. Adieu, my dear Madam.

Your's very affectionately, etc.

LETTER LVII.

To Mr. Pope,

I HAVE been running about Paris at a strange rate with my sister, and strange sights have we seen. They are, at least, strange sights to me; for, after having been accustomed to the gravity of Turks, I can scarce look with an easy and familiar aspect at the levity and agility of the airy phantoms that are dancing about me here; and I often think that I am at a puppet-shew, amidst the representations of real life. I stare prodigiously, but no body remarks it, for every body stares here; staring is à-la-mode—there is a stare of attention and *interêt*, a stare of curiosity, a stare of expectation, a stare of surprise; and it will greatly amuse you to see what trifling objects excite all this staring. This staring would have rather a solemn kind of air, were it not alleviated by grinning; for at the end of a stare, there comes always a grin; and very commonly, the entrance of a gentleman or lady into a room, is accompanied with a grin, which is designed to express complacence and social pleasure, but really shews nothing more than a certain contortion of muscles, that must make a stranger laugh really, as they laugh artificially. The French grin is equally remote from the cheerful serenity of a smile, and the cordial mirth of an honest English horse-laugh. I shall not perhaps stay here long enough to form a just idea of French manners and characters, though this I believe would require but little study, as there are no great depths in either. It appears on a superficial view, to be a frivolous, restless, and agreeable people. The abbot is my guide, and I could not easily light uppon a better; he tells me, that here the women form the character of the men; and I am convinced in the persuasion of this, by every company into which I enter. There seems here to be no intermediate state between infancy and manhood; for as soon as the boy has quit his leading-strings, he is set agog in the world; the ladies are his tutors, they make the first impressions, which generally remain, and they render the men ridiculous, by the imitation of their humours and graces; fo that dignity in manners, is a rare thing here before the age of sixty. Does not King David say somewhere, that *Man walketh in a vain shew?* I think he does; and I am sure this is peculiarly true of the Frenchman—but he walks merrily, and seems to enjoy the vision; and may he not therefore be esteemed more happy than many of our solid thinkers, whose brows are furrowed by deep reflection, and whose wisdom is so often clothed with a misty mantle of spleen and vapours?

What delights me most here, is a view of the magnificence, often accompanied with taste, that reigns in the King's palaces and gardens; for tho' I don't admire much the architecture, in which there is great irregularity and want of proportion, yet the statues, paintings, and other decorations, afford me high entertainment. One of the pieces of antiquity that struck me most in the gardens of Verfailles, was the famous Coloffean ftatue of Jupiter, the workmanfhip of Myron, which Mark Anthony carried away from Samos, and Auguflus ordered to be placed in the Capitol. It is of Parian marble; and though it has fuffered in the ruin of time, it ftill preferves ftriking lines of majefty. But furely, if marble could feel, the god would frown with a generous indignation, to fee himfelf tranfported from the Capitol into a French garden; and, after having received the homage of the Roman Emperors, who laid their laurels at his feet when they returned from their conquefts, to behold now nothing but frizzled beaus paffing by him with indifference.

I propofe fetting out foon from this place, fo that you are to expect no more letters from this fide of the water; befides, I am hurried to death, and my head swims with that vast variety of objects which I am obliged to view with such rapidity, the shortness of my time not allowing me to examine them at my leisure. There is here an excessive prodigality of ornaments and decorations, that is just the opposite extreme to what appears in our royal gardens; this prodigality is owing to the levity and inconstancy of the French taste, which always pants after something new, and thus heaps ornament upon ornament, without end or measure. It is time, however, that I should put an end to my letter; so I wish you good night,

And am, etc.

LETTER LVIII.

To Count ——.

(Tranflated from the French.)

I AM charmed, Sir, with your obliging letter; and you may perceive, by the largenefs of my paper, that I intend to give punctual anfwers to all your queftions, at leaft if my French will permit me; for, as it is a language I do not underftand to perfection, fo I much fear, that, for want of expreffions, I fhall be quickly obliged to finifh. Keep in mind, therefore, that I am writing in a foreign language; and be fure to attribute all the impertinences and triflings dropping from my pen, to the want of proper words for declaring my thoughts, but by no means to dulnefs, or natural levity.

Thefe conditions being thus agreed and fettled, I begin with telling you, that you have a true notion of the alcoran, concerning which, the Greek priests (who are the greatest scoundrels in the universe) have invented, out of their own heads, a thousand ridiculous stories, in order to decry the law of Mahomet; to run it down, I say, without any examination, or so much as letting the people read it; being afraid, that if once they began to sift the defects of the alcoran, they might not stop there, but proceed to make use of their judgment about their own legends and fictions. In effect, there is nothing so like as the fables of the Greeks and of the Mahometans; and the last have multitudes of Saints, at whose tombs miracles are by them said to be daily performed; nor are the accounts of the lives of those blessed musselmans much less stuffed with extravagances, than the spiritual romances of the Greek papas.

As to your next inquiry, I assure you,

'tis certainly falfe, though commonly believed in our parts of the world, that Mahomet excludes women from any fhare in a future happy ftate. He was too much a gentleman, and loved the fair fex too well, to ufe them fo barbaroufly. On the contrary, he promifes a very fine paradife to the Turkifh women. He fays, indeed, that this paradife will be a feparate place from that of their hufbands; but I fancy the moft part of them won't like it the worfe for that; and that the regret of this feparation, will not render their paradife the lefs agreeable. It remains to tell you, that the virtues which Mahomet requires of the women, to merit the enjoyment of future happinefs, are, not to live in fuch a manner as to become ufelefs to the world, but to employ themfelves, as much as poffible, in making little Muffulmans. The virgins, who die virgins, and the widows who marry not again, dying in mortal sin, are excluded out of paradise: for women, says he, not being capable to manage the affairs of state, nor to support the fatigues of war, God has not ordered them to govern or reform the world; but he has intrusted them with an office which is not less honourable, even that of multiplying the human race: and such as, out of malice or laziness, do not make it their business to bear or to breed children, fulfil not the duty of their vocation, and rebel against the commands of God. Here are maxims for you, prodigiously contrary to those of your convents. What will become of your St. Catharines, your St. Theresas, your St. Claras, and the whole bead-roll of your holy virgins and widows; who, if they are to be judged by this system of virtue, will be found to have been infamous creatures, that passed their whole lives in most abominable libertinism.

I know not what your thoughts may be, concerning a doctrine so extraordinary with respect to us; but I can truly inform you, Sir, that the Turks are not so ignorant as we fancy them to be in matters of politics, or philosophy, or even of gallantry. 'Tis true, that military discipline, such as now practiſed in Chriſtendom, does not mightily suit them. A long peace has plunged them into an universal sloth. Content with their condition, and accustomed to boundless luxury, they are become great enemies to all manner of fatigues. But, to make amends, the sciences flourish among them. The Effendis (that is to say, the learned) do very well deserve this name. They have no more faith in the inspiration of Mahomet, than in the infallibility of the Pope. They make a frank profession of Deism among themselves, or to those they can trust, and never speak of their law but as of a politic institution, fit now to be observed by wife men, however at first introduced by politicians and enthusiasts.

If I remember right, I think I have told you, in some former letter, that, at Belgrade, we lodged with a great and rich Effendi, a man of wit and learning, and of a very agreeable humour. We were in his house about a month, and he did constantly eat with us, drinking wine without any scruple. As I rallied him a little on this subject, he answered me, smiling, that all creatures in the world were made for the pleasure of man; and that God would not have let the vine grow, were it a sin to taste of its juice; but that, nevertheless, the law, which forbids the use of it to the vulgar, was very wise, because such sort of folks have not sense enough to take it with moderation. This Effendi appeared no stranger to the parties that prevail among us: nay, he seemed to have some knowledge of our religious disputes, and even of our writers; and I was surprised to hear him ask, among other things, how Mr. Toland did?

My paper, large as it is, draws towards an end. That I may not go beyond its limits, I must leap from religions to tulips, concerning which you ask me news. Their mixture produces surprising effects. But, what is to be observed most surprising, are the experiments of which you speak concerning animals, and which are tried here every day. The suburbs of Pera, Tophana, and Galata, are collections of strangers from all countries of the universe. They have so often intermarried, that this forms several races of people, the oddest imaginable. There is not one single family of natives, that can value itself on being unmixed. You frequently see a person, whose father was born a Grecian, the mother an Italian, the grandfather a Frenchman, the grandmother an Armenian, and their anceſtors Engliſh, Muſcovites, Aſiatics, etc.

This mixture produces creatures more extraordinary than you can imagine; nor could I ever doubt, but there were ſeveral different ſpecies of men; ſince the whites, the woolly and the long-haired blacks, the ſmall-eyed Tartars and Chineſe, the beardleſs Braſilians, and (to name no more) the oily-ſkinned yellow Nova Zemblians, have as ſpecific differences, under the ſame general kind, as greyhounds, maſtiffs, ſpaniels, bull-dogs, or the race of my little Diana, if no body is offended at the compariſon. Now, as the various intermixing of theſe latter animals cauſes mongrels, ſo mankind have their mongrels too, divided and ſubdivided into endleſs ſorts. We have daily proofs of it here, as I told you before. In the ſame animal is not seldom remarked the Greek perfidiousness, the Italian diffidence, the Spanish arrogance, the French loquacity, and, all of a sudden, he is seized with a fit of English thoughtfulness, bordering a little upon dulness, which many of us have inherited from the stupidity of our Saxon progenitors. But the family which charms me most, is that which proceeds from the fantastical conjunction of a Dutch male with a Greek female. As these are natures opposite in extremes, 'tis a pleasure to observe how the differing atoms are perpetually jarring together in the children, even so as to produce effects visible in their external form. They have the large black eyes of the country, with the fat, white, fishy flesh of Holland, and a lively air, streaked with dulness. At one and the same time, they shew that love of expensiveness, so universal among the Greeks, and an inclination to the Dutch frugality. To give an example of this, young women ruin themselves, to purchase jewels for adorning their heads, while they have not the heart to buy new shoes, or rather slippers for their feet, which are commonly in a tattered condition; a thing so contrary to the taste of our English women, that it is for shewing how neatly their feet are dressed, and for shewing this only, they are so passionately enamoured with their hoop petticoats. I have abundance of other singularities to communicate to you; but I am at the end, both of my French and my paper.

CONCERNING

Monſieur de la ROCHEFOUCAULT's Maxim: „ *That marriage is ſometimes* „ *convenient but never delightful.*"

IT may be thought a preſumptuous attempt in me to controvert a maxim advanced by ſuch a celebrated genius as Monſieur Rocheſoucault, and received with ſuch implicit faith by a nation which boaſts of ſuperior politeneſs to the reſt of the world, and which, for a long time paſt, has preſcribed the rules of gallantry to all Europe.

Nevertheleſs, prompted by that ardour which truth inſpires, I dare to maintain the contrary, and reſolutely inſiſt, that there are ſome marriages formed by love, which may be delightful, where the affections are ſympathetic. Nature has preſented us with pleaſures ſuitable to our ſpecies, and we need only to follow her impulſe, refined by taſte, and exalted by a lively and agreeable imagination, in order to attain the moſt perfect felicity of which human nature is ſuſceptible. Ambition, avarice, vanity, when enjoyed in the moſt exquiſite perfection, can yield but trifling and taſteleſs pleaſures; which will be too inconſiderable to affect a mind of delicate ſenſibility.

We may conſider the gifts of fortune as ſo many ſteps neceſſary to arrive at felicity, which we can never attain, being obliged to ſet bounds to our deſires, and being only gratified with ſome of her frivolous favours, which are nothing more than the torments of life; when they are conſidered as the neceſſary means to acquire or preſerve a more exquiſite felicity.

This felicity confiſts alone in friendſhip, founded on mutual eſteem, fixed by gratitude, ſupported by inclination, and animated by the tender ſolicitudes of

Love, whom the ancients have admirably defcribed under the appearance of a beautiful infant: It is pleafed with infantine amufements; it is delicate and affectionate, incapable of mifchief, delighted with trifles; its pleafures are gentle and innocent.

They have given a very different reprefentation of another paffion, too grofs to be mentioned, but of which alone men, in general, are fufceptible. This they have defcribed under the figure of a fatyr, who has more of the brute than of the man in his compofition. By this fabulous animal they have expreffed a paffion, which is the real foundation of all the fine exploits of modifh gallantry, and which only endeavours to glut its appetite with the poffeffion of the object which is moft lovely in its eftimation: A paffion founded in injuftice, fupported by deceit, and attended by crimes, remorfe, jealoufy.

and contempt. Can such an affection be delightful to a virtuous mind? Nevertheless, such is the delightful attendant on all illicit engagements; gallants are obliged to abandon all those sentiments of honour which are inseparable from a liberal education, and are doomed to live wretchedly in the constant pursuit of what reason condemns, to have all their pleasures embittered by remorse, and to be reduced to the deplorable condition of having renounced virtue, without being able to make vice agreeable.

It is impossible to taste the delights of love in perfection, but in a well assorted marriage; nothing betrays such a narrowness of mind as to be governed by words. What though custom, for which good reasons may be assigned, has made the words *husband* and *wife* somewhat ridiculous? A husband, in common acceptation, signifies a jealous brute, a surly tyrant; or, at best, a weak fool, who may be made to believe any thing. A wife is a domeſtic termagant, who is deſtined to deceive or torment the poor devil of a huſband. The conduct of married people, in general, ſufficiently juſtifies theſe two characters.

But, as I ſaid before, why ſhould words impoſe upon us? A well regulated marriage is not like theſe connexions of intereſt or ambition. A fond couple, attached to each other by mutual affection, are two lovers wo live happily together. Though the prieſt pronounces certain words, though the lawyer draws up certain inſtruments; yet I look on theſe preparatives in the ſame light as a lover confiders a rope-ladder which he faſtens to his miſtreſs's window: If they can but live together, what does it ſignify at what price, or by what means, their union is accompliſhed. Where love is real, and well founded, it is impoſſible to be happy but in the quiet enjoyment of the beloved object; and the price at which it is obtained, does not lessen the vivacity and delights of a passion, such as my imagination conceives. If I was inclined to romance, I would not picture images of true happiness in Arcadia. I am not prudish enough to confine the delicacy of affection to wishes only. I would open my romance with the marriage of a couple united by sentiment, taste and inclination. Can we conceive a higher felicity, than the blending of their interests and lives in such an union? The lover has the pleasure of giving his mistress the last testimony of esteem and confidence; and she, in return, commits her peace and liberty to his protection. Can they exchange more dear and affectionate pledges? Is it not natural, to give the most incontestible proofs of that tenderness with which our minds are impressed? I am sensible, that some are so nice as to maintain, that the pleasures of love are derived from the dangers and difficulties with which it is attended; they very pertly observe, that a rose would not be a rose without thorns. There are thousand insipid remarks of this sort, which make so little impression on me, that I am persuaded, was I a lover, the dread of injuring my mistress would make me unhappy, if the enjoyment of her was attended with danger to herself.

Two married lovers lead very different lives: They have the pleasure to pass their time in a successive intercourse of mutual obligations and marks of benevolence; and they have the delight to find, that each forms the entire happiness of the beloved object. Herein consists perfect felicity. The most trivial concerns of oeconomy become noble and elegant, when they are exalted by sentiments of affection; to furnish an apartment, is not barely to furnish an apartment; it is a place where I expect my lover: to prepare a supper, is not merely giving orders to my cook; it is an amusement to regale the object I dote on. In this light a woman considers these necessary occupations, as more lively and affecting pleasures than those gaudy sights which amuse the greater part of the sex, who are incapable of true enjoyment.

A fixed and affectionate attachment softens every emotion of the soul, and renders every object agreeable which presents itself to the happy lover (I mean one who is married to his mistress.) If he exercises any employment, the fatigues of the camp, the troubles of the court, all become agreeable, when he reflects, that he endures these inconveniences to serve the object of his affections. If fortune is favourable to him, (for success does not depend on merit) all the advantages it procures, are so many tributes which he thinks due to the charms of the lovely fair; and, in gratifying this ambition, he feels a more lively pleafure, and more worthy of an honeft man, than that of raifing his fortune, and gaining public applaufe. He enjoys glory, titles, and riches, no farther than as they regard her he loves; and when he attracts the approbation of a fenate, the applaufe of an army, or the commendation of his prince, it is her praifes which ultimately flatter him.

In a referve of fortune, he has the confolation of retiring to one who is affected by his difgrace; and, locked in her embraces, he has the fatisfaction of giving utterance to the following tender reflections: ,, My happinefs does not de‑
,, pend on the caprice of fortune; I have
,, a conftant afylum againft inquietude.
,, Your efteem renders me infenfible of
,, the injuftice of a court, or the ingra‑
,, titude of a mafter; and my loffes afford
,, me a kind of pleafure, fince they fur‑

„ nifh me with frefh proofs of your vir-
„ tue and affection. Of what ufe is gran-
„ deur to thofe who are already happy? We
„ have no need of flatterers, we want no
„ equipages; I reign in your affections,
„ and I enjoy every delight in the poffef-
„ fion of your perfon."

In fhort, there is no fituation in which melancholy may not be affuaged by the company of the beloved object. Sicknefs itfelf is not without its alleviation, when we have the pleafure of being attended by her we love. I fhould never conclude, if I attempted to give a detail of all the delights of an attachment, wherein we meet with every thing which can flatter the fenfes with the moft lively and diffufive raptures. But I muft not omit taking notice of the pleafure of beholding the lovely pledges of a tender friendfhip, daily growing up, and of amufing ourfelves, according to our different fexes, in training them to perfection. We give way to this agreeable inftinct of nature, refined by love. In a daughter, we praife the beauty of her mother; in a fon, we commend the underftanding, and the appearance of innate probity which we efteem in his father. It is a pleafure which, according to Mofes, the Almighty himfelf enjoyed, when he beheld the work of his hands, and faw that all was good.

Speaking of Mofes, I cannot forbear obferving, that the primitive plan of felicity infinitely furpaffes all others; and I cannot form an idea of paradife, more like a paradife, than the ftate in which our firft parents were placed. That proved of fhort duration, becaufe they were unacquainted with the world; and it is for the fame reafon, that fo few lovematches prove happy. Eve was like a filly child, and Adam was not much enlightened. When fuch people come together, their being amorous is to no purpofe, for their affections muft necef-

farily be short-lived. In the transports of
their love, they form supernatural ideas
of each other. The man thinks his mistress an angel, because she is handsome;
and she is enraptured with the merit of
her lover, because he adores her. The
first decay of her complexion deprives
her of his adoration, and the husband,
being no longer an adorer, becomes hateful to her who had no other foundation
for her love. By degrees, they grow dis-
gustful to each other; and, after the
example of our first parents, they do
not fail to reproach each other with the
crime of their mutual imbecility. After
indifference, contempt comes apace, and
they are convinced, that they must hate
each other, because they are married.
Their smallest defects swell in each other's
view, and they grow blind to those
charms, which in any other object, would
affect them. A commerce founded merely

on sensation, can be attended with no other consequences.

A man, when he marries the object of his affections, should forget that she appears to him adorable, and should consider her merely as a mortal, subject to disorders, caprice, and ill temper; he should arm himself with fortitude, to bear the loss of her beauty, and should provide himself with a fund of complaisance, which is requisite to support a constant intercourse with a person, even of the highest understanding and the greatest equanimity. The wife, on the other hand, should not expect a continued course of adulation and obedience; she should dispose herself to obey in her turn with a good grace: a science very difficult to attain, and consequently the more estimable in the opinion of a man who is sensible of the merit. She should endeavour to revive the charms of the mistress, by the solidity and good sense of the friend.

When a pair who entertain such rational sentiments, are united by indissoluble bonds, all nature smiles upon them, and the most common objects appear delightful. In my opinion, such a life is infinitely more happy and more voluptuous, than the most ravishing and best regulated gallantry.

A woman who is capable of reflection, can consider a gallant in no other light, than that of a seducer, who would take advantage of her weakness, to procure a momentary pleasure, at the expence of her glory, her peace, her honour, and, perhaps, her life. A highwayman who claps a pistol to your breast, to rob you of your purse, is less dishonest and less guilty; and I have so good an opinion of myself, as to believe, that if I was a man, I should be as capable of assuming the character of an assassin, as that of defiling an honest woman, esteemed in the world, and happy in her husband, by infpiring her with a paffion, to which fhe muft facrifice her honour, her tranquillity and her virtue.

Should I make her defpicable, who appears amiable in my eyes? Should I reward her tendernefs, by making her abhorred by her family, by rendering her children indifferent to her, and her hufband deteftable? I believe that thefe reflections would have appeared to me in as ftrong a light, if my fex had not rendered them excufable in fuch cafes; and I hope, that I fhould have had more fenfe, than to imagine vice the lefs vicious, becaufe it is the fafhion.

N. B. I am much pleafed with the Turkifh manners; a people, though ignorant, yet, in my judgment, extremely polite. A gallant, convicted of having debauched a married woman, is regarded as a pernicious being, and held in the fame abhorrence as a proftitute with us. He is certain of never making his fortune; and they would deem it scandalous to confer any considerable employment on a man suspected of having committed such enormous injustice.

What would these moral people think of our anti-knightserrant, who are ever in pursuit of adventures to reduce innocent virgins to distress, and to rob virtuous women of their honour; who regard beauty, youth, rank, nay virtue itself, as so many incentives, which inflame their desires, and render their efforts more eager; and who, priding themselves in the glory of appearing expert seducers, forget, that with all their endeavours, they can only acquire the second rank in that noble order, the devil having long since been in possession of the first.

Our barbarous manners are so well calculated for the establishment of vice and wretchedness, which are ever inseparable, that it requires a degree of understanding and sensibility, infinitely above the common, to relish the felicity of a marriage such as I have described. Nature is so weak, and so prone to change, that it is difficult to maintain the best grounded constancy, in the midst of those dissipations, which our ridiculous customs have rendered unavoidable.

It must pain an amorous husband, to see his wife take all the fashionable liberties; it seems harsh not to allow them; and, to be conformable, he is reduced to the necessity of letting every one take them that will, to hear her impart the charms of her understanding to all the world, to see her display her bosom at noon-day, to behold her bedeck herself for the ball, and for the play, and attract a thousand and a thousand adorers, and listen to the insipid flattery of a thousand and a thousand coxcombs. Is it possible to preserve an esteem for such a creature? or, at least, must not her value be greatly diminished by such a commerce?

I must still resort to the maxims of the East, where the most beautiful women are content to confine the power of their charms to him who has a right to enjoy them; and they are too sincere, not to confess, that they think themselves capable of exciting desires.

I recollect a conversation that I had with a lady of great quality at Constantinople, (the most amiable woman I ever knew in my life, and with whom I afterwards contracted the closest friendship.) She frankly acknowledged, that she was satisfied with her husband. What libertines, said she, you Christian ladies are! You are permitted to receive visits from as many men as you think proper, and your laws allow you the unlimited use of love and wine. I assured her, that she was wrong informed, and that it was criminal to liſten to, or to love, any other than our huſbands. „Your „huſbands are great fools, ſhe replied „ſmiling, to be content with ſo precarious „a fidelity. Your necks, your eyes, your „hands, your converſation are all for the „public, and what do you pretend to re- „ſerve for them? Pardon me, my pretty „Sultana, ſhe added, embracing me, I „have a ſtrong inclination to believe all „that you tell me, but you would im- „poſe impoſſibilities upon me. I know „the filthineſs of the infidels; I perceive „that you are aſhamed, and I will ſay „no more."

I found ſo much good ſenſe and propriety in what ſhe ſaid, that I knew not how to contradict her; and, at length, I acknowledged, that ſhe had reaſon to prefer the Mahometan manners to our ridiculous cuſtoms, which form a confuſed medley of the rigid maxims of Chriſtianity, with all the libertiniſm of the Spartans: and, notwithstanding our absurd manners, I am persuaded, that a woman who is determined to place her happiness in her husband's affections, should abandon the extravagant desire of engaging public adoration; and that a husband, who tenderly loves his wife, should, in his turn, give up the reputation of being a gallant. You find that I am supposing a very extraordinary pair; it is not very surprising, therefore, that such an union should be uncommon in those countries, where it is requisite to conform to established customs, in order to be happy.

VERSES,

Written in the Chiosk at Pera, overlooking Constantinople, December 26th, 1718.

By Lady
MARY WORTLEY MONTAGUE.

GIVE me, great God! said I, a little farm,
In summer shady, and in winter warm;
Where a clear spring gives birth to murm'ring brooks,
By nature gliding down the mossy rocks.
Not artfully by leaden pipes convey'd,
Or greatly falling in a forc'd *cascade*,
Pure and unsully'd winding thro' the shade.
All-bounteous Heaven has added to my pray'r
A softer climate, and a purer air.

Our frozen isle now chilling winter binds,
Deform'd by rains, and rough with blast-
ing winds;
The wither'd woods grow white with
hoary frost,
By driving storms their verdant beauty
lost;
The trembling birds their leafless covert
shun,
And seek, in distant climes a warmer sun:
The water-nymphs their silent urns de-
plore,
Ev'n *Thames* benum'd's a river now no
more:
The barren meads no longer yield de-
light,
By glist'ring snows made painful to the
sight.
Here summer reigns with one eternal
smile,
Succeeding harvests bless the happy soil.
Fair fertile fields, to whom indulgent
Heaven

Has ev'ry charm of ev'ry feafon given;
No killing cold deforms the beauteous
year,
The fpringing flowers no coming winter
fear.
But as the parent *Rofe* decays and dies,
The infant-buds with brighter colour
rife,
And with frefh fweets the mother's fcent
fupplies.
Near them the *Violet* grows with odours
bleft,
And blooms in more than Tyrian purple
dreft;
The rich *Jonquils* their golden beams
difplay,
And fhine in glories emulating day;
The peaceful groves their verdant leaves
retain,
The ftreams ftill murmur, undefil'd with
rain,
And tow'ring greens adorn the fruitful
plain,

The warbling kind uninterrupted fing,
Warm'd with enjoyments of perpetual
  spring.
Here, at my window, I at once survey
The crowded city and resounding sea;
In distant views the *Asian* mountains rise,
And lose their snowy summits in the skies;
Above those mountains proud *Olympus*
  towers,
The parliamental seat of heavenly powers.
New to the sight, my ravish'd eyes admire
Each gilded crescent and each antique
  spire,
The marble mosques, beneath whose
  ample domes
Fierce warlike *Sultans* sleep in peaceful
  tombs;
Those lofty structures, once the Chris-
  tians' boast,
Their names, their beauty, and their
  honours lost;
Those altars bright with gold and sculp-
  ture grac'd,

By barb'rous zeal of savage foes defac'd,
Sophia alone her ancient name retains,
Tho' unbelieving vows her shrine pro-
   fanes;
Where holy Saints have died in sacred
   cells,
Where Monarchs pray'd, the frantic
   Dervise dwells.
How art thou fall'n, imperial city, low!
Where are thy hopes of *Roman* glory
   now?
Where are thy palaces by prelates
   rais'd?
Where *Grecian* artists all their skill
   display'd,
Before the happy sciences decay'd;
So vast, that youthful Kings might here
   reside,
So splendid, to content a Patriarch's
   pride;
Convents where Emperors profess'd of
   old,
Their labour'd pillars that their triumphs
   told;

Vain monuments of them that once were
    great,
' Sunk undistinguish'd by one common fate;
One little spot, the tenure small contains,
Of *Greek* nobility, the poor remains.
Where other *Helens* with like pow'rful
    charms,
Had once engag'd the warring world in
    arms;
Those names which royal ancestors can
    boast,
In mean mechanic arts obscurely lost;
Those eyes a second *Homer* might inspire,
Fix'd at the loom destroy their useless fire.
  Griev'd at a view which struck upon
    my mind
The short-liv'd vanity of human kind,
In gaudy objects I indulge my sight,
And turn where *Eastern pomp* gives
    gay delight;
See the vast train in various habits drest,
By the bright scimitar and sable vest,
The proud vizier distinguish'd o'er the
    rest;

Six slaves in gay attire his bridle hold,
His bridle rich with gems, and stirrups
gold;
His snowy steed adorn'd with costly pride,
Whole troops of soldiers mounted by
his side,
These top the plumy crest *Arabian*
courtiers guide.
With artful duty, all decline their eyes,
No bellowing shouts of noisy crowds arise;
Silence, in solemn state, the march attends,
Till at the dread *Divan* the slow pro-
cession ends.

Yet not these prospects all profusely gay,
The gilded navy that adorns the sea,
The rising city in confusion fair,
Magnificently form'd irregular;
Where woods and palaces at once
surprise,
Gardens on gardens, domes on domes
arise,
And endless beauties tire the wand'ring
eyes;

So sooth my wishes, or so charm my
        mind,
As this *retreat* secure from human-kind.
No knave's successful craft does spleen
        excite,
No coxcomb's tawdry splendour shocks
        my sight;
No mob-alarm awakes my female fear,
No praise my mind, nor envy hurts
        my ear,
Ev'n fame itself can hardly reach me
        here:
Impertinence with all her tattling train,
Fair-sounding flattery's delicious bane;
Censorious folly, noisy party-rage,
The thousand tongues with which she
        must engage,
Who dares have *virtue* in a *vicious age.*

VERSES,

TO THE LADY

MARY WORTLEY MONTAGUE,

BY

Mr. POPE.

  IN beauty or wit,
  No mortal as yet
To queſtion your empire has dar'd.
  But men of diſcerning
  Have thought that in learning,
To yield to a lady was hard.

  Impertinent ſchools,
  With muſty dull rules
Have reading to females deny'd;
  So Papiſts refuſe
  The BIBLE to uſe,
Leſt flocks ſhould be wiſe as their guide.

'Twas a woman at firſt
(Indeed ſhe was curſt)
In *knowledge* that taſted *delight;*
And ſages agree,
The laws ſhould decree
To the firſt poſſeſſor the right.

Then bravely, fair dame,
Renew the old claim,
Which to your whole ſex does belong,
And let men receive,
From a ſecond bright Eve,
The knowledge of *right* and of *wrong.*

But if the firſt Eve
Hard doom did receive,
When only *one apple* had ſhe,
What a puniſhment new
Shall be found out for you,
Who taſting have robb'd the *whole tree?*

THE POETICAL WORKS

OF THE

RIGHT HONOURABLE

LADY MARY WORTLEY

MONTAGUE.

VOLUME V.

CONTENTS.

Page.

Town Eclogues 165
Verses addressed to the Imitator of the first Satire of the Second Book of Horace 208
An Epistle to Lord B. 219
An Epistle from Arthur Grey the Footman 225
An Answer to a Love-Letter. 234
An Elegy on Mrs. Thomson. 237
Answer to a Lady, who advised Retirement. 239
On the Death of Mrs. Bowes. ... 240
Verses written in a Garden. 242
A Hymn to the Moon. 243
Epilogue to Mary Queen of Scots 244
A Ballad. 247
The Lover, a Ballad. 250

	Page.
The Lady's Resolve.	254
The Gentleman's Answer.	255
A Man in Love.	256
A Receipt to cure the Vapours.	257
The Fifth Ode of Horace imitated.	259
Farewell to Bath.	260
To Clio.	262
A Caveat to the Fair Sex.	265

TOWN ECLOGUES*).

MONDAY.

ROXANA, or, the *Drawing-Room.*

ROXANA from the Court retiring late,
Sigh'd her soft sorrows at *St. James's*
   gate.
Such heavy thoughts lay brooding in
   her breast,
Not her own chairmen with more weight
   oppress'd;
They groan the cruel load they're doom'd
   to bear;
She in these gentle sounds express'd her
   care.

*) Of these six Eclogues, four only were written by Lady Mary Wortley Montague. Thursday the *Bassette Table*, and Friday the *Toilette*, being the Productions of Mr. Pope and Mr. Gay.

„ Was it for this, that I those roses
wear,
„ For this new, set the jewels for my
hair?
„ Ah! princess! with what zeal have I
pursu'd!
„ Almost forgot the duty of a prude.
„ Thinking I never could attend too
soon,
„ I've miss'd my prayers, to get me
dress'd by noon.
„ For thee, ah! what for thee did I
resign?
„ My pleasures, passions, all that e'er
was mine.
„ I sacrific'd both modesty and ease,
„ Left operas, and went to filthy plays;
„ Double entendres shock'd my tender
ear,
„ Yet even this for thee I chose to bear.
„ In glowing youth, when nature bids
be gay,
„ And every joy of life before me lay,

„By honour prompted, and by pride
  reſtrain'd,
„The pleaſures of the young my ſoul
  diſdain'd:
„Sermons I ſought, and with a mien
  ſevere
„Cenſur'd my neighbours, and ſaid
  daily pray'r.
„Alas! how chang'd!—with the ſame
  ſermon-mien
„That once I pray'd, the *What-d'ye-
  call't* *) I've ſeen.
„Ah! cruel princeſs, for thy ſake I've
  loſt
„That reputation which ſo dear had
  coſt:
„I, who avoided every public place,
„When bloom and beauty bade me ſhew
  my face;
„Now near thee conſtant every night
  abide

*) A Farce, by Mr. Gay.

,, With never-failing duty by the fide,
,, Myfelf and daughters ftanding on a row,
,, To all the foreigners a goodly fhew!
,, Oft had your drawing-room been fadly
thin,
,, And merchants' wives clofe by the
chair been feen;
,, Had not I amply fill'd the empty
fpace,
,, And fav'd your highnefs from the dire
difgrace.
,, Yet *Coquetilla's* artifice prevails,
,, When all my merit and my duty fails:
,, That *Coquetilla*, whofe deluding airs
,, Corrupts our virgins, and our youth
enfnares;
,, So funk her character, fo loft her fame,
,, Scarce vifited before your highnefs
came:
,, Yet for the bed-chamber 'tis her you
chufe,
,, When Zeal and Fame and Virtue you
refufe.

„Ah! worthy choice! not one of all
  your train
„Whom cenfure blafts not, and difho-
  nours ftain.
„Let the nice hind now fuckle dirty
  pigs,
„And the proud pea-hen hatch the cuc-
  koo's eggs!
„Let *Iris* leave her paint and own her
  age,
„And grave *Suffolka* wed a giddy page!
„A greater miracle is daily view'd,
„A virtuous princefs with a court fo
  lewd.
„I know thee, Court! with all thy
  treach'rous wiles,
„Thy falfe careffes and undoing fmiles!
„Ah! princefs, learn'd in all the courtly
  arts
„To cheat our hopes, and yet to gain
  our hearts!
„Large lovely bribes are the great
  ftatefman's aim;

„ And the neglected patriot follows fame.
„ The prince is ogled; some the king
purfue;
„ But your *Roxana* only follows *You*.
„ Despis'd *Roxana*, cease, and try to find
„ Some other, since the princefs proves
unkind:
„ Perhaps it is not hard to find at
court,
„ If not a greater, a more firm sup-
port."

TUESDAY.

St. JAMES's Coffee-House.

SILLIANDER and PATCH.

THOU, who so many favours haft
receiv'd,
Wond'rous to tell, and hard to be believ'd,
Oh! H———d, to my lays attention lend,

Hear how two lovers boaſtingly contend:
Like thee ſuccefsful, ſuch their bloomy
youth,
Renown'd alike for gallantry and truth.
St. James's bell had toll'd ſome
wretches in,
(As tatter'd riding-hoods alone could fin)
The happier ſinners now their charms
put out,
And to their mantuas their complexions
ſuit;
The opera queens had finiſh'd half their
faces,
And city dames already taken places;
Fops of all kinds, to ſee the Lion, run;
The beauties ſtay till the firſt act's
begun,
And beaux ſtep home to put freſh
linen on.
No well-dreſs'd youth in coffee-houſe
remain'd,
But penſive *Patch*, who on the window
lean'd;

Vol. V.   P

And *Silliander*, that alert and gay,
First pick'd his teeth, and then began
   to say.

SILLIANDER.

Why all these sighs; ah! why so pen-
   five grown?
Some cause there is why thus you sit
   alone.
Does hapless passion all this sorrow
   move?
Or dost thou envy where the ladies love?

PATCH.

If, whom they love, my envy must
   pursue,
'Tis true, at least, I ever envy you.

SILLIANDER.

No, I'm unhappy—you are in the
   right—
'Tis you they favour, and 'tis me they
   slight.
Yet I could tell, but that I hate to
   boast,
A club of ladies where 'tis me they
   toast.

PATCH.
Toasting does seldom any favour prove;
Like us, they never toast the thing they
love.
A certain duke one night my health
begun;
With chearful pledges round the room
it run,
'Till the young *Silvia*, press'd to drink
it too,
Started and vow'd she knew not what
to do:
What, drink a fellow's health! she dy'd
with shame:
Yet blush'd whenever she pronounc'd
my name.

SILLIANDER.
Ill fates pursue me, may I never
find
The dice propitious, or the ladies kind,
If fair Miss *Flippy's* fan I did not tear,
And one from me she condescends to
wear.

PATCH.
Women are always ready to receive;
'Tis then a favour when the sex will
give.
A lady (but she is too great to name)
Beauteous in person, spotless in her
fame,
With gentle strugglings let me force this
ring;
Another day may give another thing.
SILLIANDER.
I could say something—see this billet-
doux—
And as for presents—look upon my
shoe——
These buckles were not forc'd, nor half
a theft,
But a young countess fondly made the
gift.
PATCH.
My countess is more nice, more art-
ful too,
Affects to fly, that I may fierce pursue:

This snuff-box which I begg'd, she still
      deny'd;
And when I strove to snatch it, seem'd
      to hide;
She laugh'd and fled, and as I sought
      to seize,
With affectation cram'd it down her
      stays;
Yet hop'd she did not place it there
      unseen.
I press'd her breasts, and pull'd it from
      between.

SILLIANDER.

Last night, as I stood ogling of her
      grace,
Drinking delicious poison from her face,
The soft enchantress did that face de-
      cline,
Nor ever rais'd her eyes to meet with
      mine;
With sudden art some secret did pretend,
Lean'd cross two chairs to whisper to a
      friend,

While the stiff whalebone with the motion rose,
And thousand beauties to my sight expose.

PATCH.

Early this morn—(but I was afk'd to
come)
I drank bohea in *Celia's* dressing-room:
Warm from her bed, to me alone
within,
Her night-gown fasten'd with a single pin;
Her night-cloaths tumbled with resistless
grace,
And her bright hair play'd careless round
her face;
Reaching the kettle made her gown unpin,
She wore no waistcoat, and her shift
was thin.

SILLIANDER.

See *Titiana* driving to the park!
Hark! let us follow, 'tis not yet too dark:
In her all beauties of the spring are seen,
Her cheeks are rosy, and her mantle
green.

PATCH.

See *Tintoretta* to the opera goes!
Haste, or the crowd will not permit our
    bows;
In her the glory of the heav'ns we view,
Her eyes are star-like, and her mantle
    blue.

SILLIANDER.

What colour does in *Celia's* stockings
    shine?
Reveal that secret, and the prize is
    thine.

PATCH.

What are her garters? tell me if you
    can;
I'll freely own thee far the happier man.
  Thus *Patch* continued his heroic
    strain,
While *Silliander* but contends in vain,
After a conquest so important gain'd,
Unrivall'd *Patch* in every ruelle reign'd.

WEDNESDAY.

The Tête-à-Tête.

DANCINDA.

„No, fair *Dancinda*, no; you ſtrive
 in vain
„To calm my care, and mitigate my
 pain;
„If all my ſighs, my cares, can fail to
 move,
„Ah! ſooth me not with fruitleſs vows
 of love."
Thus *Strephon* ſpoke. *Dancinda* thus
 reply'd:
What muſt I do to gratify your pride?
Too well you know (ungrateful as thou
 art)
How much you triumph in this tender
 heart:
What proof of love remains for me to
 grant?
Yet ſtill you teaze me with ſome new
 complaint.

Oh! would to heaven!—but the fond
        wiſh is vain—
Too many favours had not made it
        plain!
But ſuch a paſſion breaks through all
        diſguiſe,
Love reddens on my cheek, and wiſh-
        es in my eyes.
Is't not enough (inhuman and unkind!)
I own the ſecret conflict of my mind;
You cannot know what ſecret pain I
        prove,
When I with burning bluſhes own I
        love.
You ſee my artleſs joy at your approach,
I ſigh, I faint, I tremble at your touch;
And in your abſence all the world I ſhun;
I hate mankind, and curſe the chearing
        ſun.
Still as I fly, ten thouſand ſwains purſue;
Ten thouſand ſwains I ſacrifice to you.
I ſhew you all my heart without diſ-
        guiſe:

But thefe are tender proofs that you
    defpife———
I fee too well what wifhes you purfue;
You would not only conquer, but undo:
You, cruel victor, weary of your flame,
Would feek a cure in my eternal fhame;
And not content my honour to fubdue,
Now ftrive to triumph o'er my virtue too.
Oh! *Love*, a God indeed to woman-
    kind;
Whofe arrows burn me, and whofe fet-
    ters bind,
Avenge thy altars, vindicate thy fame,
And blaft thefe traitors that profane thy
    name;
Who by pretending to thy facred fire,
Raife curfed trophies to impure defire.
 Have you forgot with what enfnar-
    ing art
You firft feduc'd this fond uncautious
    heart?
Then as I fled, did you not kneeling
    cry,

„Turn, cruel beauty; whither would
you fly?
„Why all these doubts? why this diſ-
truſtful fear?
„No impious wiſhes ſhall offend your
ear:
„Nor ever ſhall my boldeſt hopes pre-
tend
„Above the title of a tender friend;
„Bleſt, if my lovely goddeſs will permit
„My humble vows thus ſighing at her
feet.
„The tyrant Love that in my boſom
reigns,
„The god himſelf ſubmits to wear your
chains:
„You ſhall direct his courſe, his ardour
tame,
„And check the fury of his wildeſt
flame."
Unpractis'd youth is eaſily deceiv'd;
Sooth'd by ſuch ſounds, I liſten'd and
believ'd;

Now, quite forgot that soft submissive
    fear,
You dare to ask what I must blush to
    hear.
Could I forget the honour of my race,
And meet your wishes, fearless of dis-
    grace;
Could passion o'er my tender youth
    prevail,
And all my mother's pious maxims fail;
Yet to preserve your heart (which still
    must be,
False as it is, for ever dear to me)
This fatal proof of love I would not
    give,
Which you'd contemn the moment you
    receive.
The wretched she, who yields to guilty
    joys,
A man may pity, but he must despise.
Your ardour ceas'd, I then should see
    you shun
The wretched victim by your arts undone.

Yet if I could that cold indifference
bear,
What more would strike me with the
last despair,
With this reflection would my soul be
torn,
To know I merited your cruel scorn.
Has love no pleasures free from guilt
or fear?
Pleasures less fierce, more lasting, more
sincere?
Thus let us gently kiss and fondly gaze,
Love is a child, and like a child it
plays.
O *Strephon*, if you would continue
just,
If love be something more than brutal
lust,
Forbear to ask what I must still deny,
This bitter pleasure, this destructive joy,
So closely follow'd by the dismal train
Of cutting shame and guilt's heart-pierc-
ing pain.

She paus'd, and fix'd her eyes upon
her fan;
He took a pinch of snuff, and thus began:
Madam, if love—but he could say no
more,
For Mademoiselle came rapping at the
door.
The dangerous moments no adieus afford;
—Begone, she cries, I'm sure I hear
my lord.
The lover starts from his unfinish'd
loves,
To snatch his hat, and seek his scat-
ter'd gloves:
The sighing dame to meet her dear pre-
pares,
While *Strephon* cursing slips down the
back-stairs.

THURSDAY.

THE BASSETTE-TABLE *).

SMILINDA and CARDELIA.

CARDELIA.

THE *Bassette-table* spread, the Tallier come;
Why stays *Smilinda* in the dressing-room?
Rise, pensive nymph! the tallier waits for you.

SMILINDA.

Ah! madam, since my *Sharper* is untrue,
I joyless make my once ador'd *alpieu*.

---

*) Only this, of all the Town Eclogues, was Mr. Pope's, and is here printed from a copy corrected by his own hand. The humour of it lies in this happy circumstance, that the one is in love with the Game, and the other with the Sharper.

I saw him stand behind *Ombrelia's*
   chair,
And whisper with that soft, deluding
   air,
And those feign'd sighs, which cheat
   the list'ning fair.

   CARDELIA.
Is this the cause of your romantic
   strains?
A mightier grief my heavier heart sus-
   tains.
As you by Love, so I by Fortune cross'd;
One, one bad *deal* three *septleva's* have
   lost.

   SMILINDA.
Is that the grief which you compare
   with mine?
With ease the smiles of Fortune I resign:
Would all my gold in one bad *deal*
   were gone;
Were lovely *Sharper* mine, and mine
   alone.

CARDELIA.
A lover loſt is but a common care;
And prudent nymphs againſt that change
prepare.
The knave of clubs thrice loſt: oh! who
could gueſs
This fatal ſtroke! this unforeſeen diſtreſs?
SMILINDA.
See! *Betty Loveit* very *à propos*,
She all the care of *love* and *play* does
know;
Dear *Betty* ſhall th' important point
decide,
Betty, who oft the pain of each has
try'd;
Impartial, ſhe ſhall ſay who ſuffers moſt,
By *cards' ill uſage*, or by *lovers loſt*.
LOVEIT.
Tell, tell your griefs; attentive will
I ſtay,
Though time is precious, and I want
ſome tea.

CARDELIA.

Behold this *equipage*, by *Mathers* wrought,
With fifty guineas (a great pen'orth!) bought.
See on the tooth-pick, *Mars* and *Cupid* strive!
And both the struggling figures seem alive.
Upon the bottom shines the queen's bright face;
A myrtle foliage round the thimble case.
Jove, *Jove* himself, does on the scissars shine;
The metal, and the workmanship divine!

SMILINDA.

This *snuff-box*, once the pledge of *Sharper's* love,
When rival beauties for the present strove;
At *Corticelli's* he the raffle won;
Then first his passion was in public shown:
Hazardia blush'd and turn'd her head aside,
A rival's envy (all in vain) to hide—

This *snuff-box*—on the hinge see bril-
    liants shine:
This *snuff-box* will I stake; the prize
    is mine.

CARDELIA.

Alas! far lesser losses than I bear,
Have made a soldier sigh, a lover swear.
And oh! what makes the disappoint-
    ment hard,
'Twas my own lord that drew the fatal
    card.
In complaisance, I took the *queen* he
    gave;
Though my own secret wish was for the
    knave.
The *knave* won *Sonica* which I had chose;
And the next *pull*, my *septleva* I lose.

SMILINDA.

But ah! what aggravates the killing
    smart,
The cruel thought that stabs me to the
    heart;
This curs'd *Ombrelia*, this undoing fair,
By whose vile arts this heavy grief I bear

She, at whose name I shed these spiteful
    tears,
She owes to me the very charms she wears:
An aukward thing when first she came
    to town;
Her shape unfashion'd, and her face
    unknown.
She was my friend, I taught her first to
    spread
Upon her sallow cheeks enlivening red.
I introduc'd her to the Park and plays;
And by my int'rest *Cosins* made her flays.
Ungrateful wretch! with mimic airs grown
    pert,
She dares to steal my favourite lover's
    heart.

CARDELIA.

Wretch that I was! how often have I
    swore,
When *Winnall* tallied, I would *punt*
    no more?
I know the bite, yet to my ruin run;
And see the folly, which I cannot shun.

SMILINDA.
How many maids have *Sharper's* vows
　　　deceiv'd?
How many curs'd the moment they be-
　　　liev'd?
Yet his known falshoods could no warn-
　　　ing prove:
Ah! what is warning to a maid in love?
　　CARDELIA.
But of what marble must that breast
　　　be form'd,
To gaze on *Bassette*, and remain un-
　　　warm'd?
When *Kings*, *Queens*, *Knaves*, are set
　　　in decent rank;
Expos'd in glorious heaps the tempting
　　　bank,
Guineas, half-guineas, all the shining
　　　train;
The winner's pleasure and the loser's pain:
In bright confusion open *rouleaus* lie,
They strike the soul, and glitter in the eye,
Fir'd by the sight, all reason I disdain;

My paſſions riſe, and will not bear the
rein.
Look upon *Baſſette*, you who reaſon
boaſt,
And ſee if reaſon muſt not *there* be loſt.
SMILINDA.
What more than marble muſt that heart
compoſe,
Can hearken coldly to my *Sharper's*
vows?
Then when he trembles, when his bluſh-
es riſe,
When awful love ſeems melting in his
eyes?
With eager beats his Mechlin cravat
moves:
He loves, I whiſper to myſelf, *he loves!*
Such unfeign'd paſſion in his looks ap-
pears,
I loſe all mem'ry of my former fears:
My panting heart confeſſes all his charms,
I yield at once, and ſink into his arms:
Think of that moment, you who pru-
dence boaſt;

For such a moment, prudence well were
lost.
CARDELIA.
At the *groom-porter's*, batter'd bul-
lies play,
Some *dukes* at Marybone bowl time
away.
But who the bowl, or rattling dice
compares
To *Baſſette's* heavenly joys, and pleaſ-
ing cares?
SMILINDA.
Soft *Simpliciett* doats upon a beau;
Prudina likes a man, and laughs at ſhow.
Their ſeveral graces in my *Sharper* meet;
Strong as the footman, as the maſter
ſweet.
LOVEIT.
Ceaſe your contention, which has been
too long;
I grow impatient, and the tea's too ſtrong.
Attend, and yield to what I now decide:
The *equipage* ſhall grace *Smilinda's* ſide;

The snuff-box to *Cardelia* I decree,
Now leave complaining, and begin your
tea.

FRIDAY.

The Toilette.

Lydia.

Now twenty springs had cloath'd the
park with green,
Since *Lydia* knew the blossoms of fifteen;
No lovers now her morning hours molest,
And catch her at her toilette half undrest.
The thund'ring knocker wakes the street
no more,
Nor chairs, nor coaches crowd the silent
door;
Nor at the window all her mornings pass,
Or at the dumb devotion of her glass:
Reclin'd upon her arm she pensive sate,
And curs'd th' inconstancy of man too late.

„Oh youth! O spring of life for ever
 loſt!
„No more my name shall reign the
 fav'rite toaſt;
„On glaſs no more the diamond grave
 my name,
„And lines miſ-ſpelt record my lover's
 flame:
„Nor shall ſide boxes watch my wan-
 d'ring eyes,
„And, as they catch the glance, in rows
 ariſe
„With humble bows; nor white-glov'd
 beaus encroach
„In crowds behind, to guard me to my
 coach.
„What shall I do to spend the hateful
 day?
„At chapel shall I wear the morn away?
„Who there appears at theſe unmodiſh
 hours,
„But ancient matrons with their frizled
 tow'rs,„

„And grey religious maids? My prefence
   there
„Amidft that fober train, would own
   defpair;
„Nor am I yet fo old, nor is my glance
„As yet fix'd wholly on devotion's
   trance.
„Strait then I'll drefs, and take my
   wonted range
„Through India fhops, to Motteux's,
   or the Change,
„Where the tall jar erects its ftately pride,
„With antic fhapes in China's azure dy'd;
„There carelefs lies a rich brocade un-
   roll'd,
„Here fhines a cabinet with burnifh'd
   gold.
„But then, alas! I muft be forc'd to pay,
„And bring no penn'orths, not a fan
   away!
„How am I curs'd, unhappy and
   forlorn!
„My lover's triumph, and my fex's
   fcorn!

„ Falſe is the pompous grief of youthful
heirs;
„ Falſe are the looſe coquet's inveigling
airs;
„ Falſe is the crafty courtier's plighted
word;
„ Falſe are the dice when gameſters ſtamp
the board;
„ Falſe is the ſprightly widow's public
tear;
„ Yet theſe to *Damon's* oaths are all
ſincere.
„ For what young flirt, baſe man, am
I abus'd?
„ To pleaſe your wife am I unkindly us'd?
„ 'Tis true, her face may boaſt the peach's
bloom;
„ But does her nearer whiſper breathe
perfume?
„ I own her taper ſhape is form'd to
pleaſe;
„ But don't you ſee her unconfin'd by
ſtays?

„ She doubly to fifteen may claim pre‑
tence;
„ Alike we read it in her face and fenfe.
„ Infipid, fervile thing! whom I difdain!
„ Her phlegm can beft fupport the mar‑
riage chain.
„ Damon is practis'd in the modifh life;
„ Can hate, and yet be civil to his wife;
„ He games, he drinks, he fwears, he
fights, he roves;
„ Yet *Cloe* can believe he fondly loves.
„ Miftrefs and wife by turns fupply his
need;
„ A mifs for pleafure, and a wife for
breed.
„ Powder'd with diamonds, free from
fpleen or care,
„ She can a fullen hufband's humour
bear;
„ Her credulous friendfhip, and her ftu‑
pid eafe,
„ Have often been my jeft in happier
days:

,, Now *Cloe* boasts and triumphs in my pains;
,, To her he's faithful; 'tis to me he feigns.
,, Am I that stupid thing to bear neglect,
,, And force a smile, not daring to suspect?
,, No, perjur'd man! a wife may be content,
,, But you shall find a mistress can resent.''
Thus love-sick *Lydia* rav'd; her maid appears,
And in her faithful hand the band-box bears;
(The Cestos that reform'd inconstant *Jove*
Not better fill'd with what allur'd to love)
,, How well this ribband's gloss becomes your face!''
She cries in rapture; ,, then, so sweet a lace!
,, How charmingly you look! so bright! so fair!
,, 'Tis to your eyes the head-dress owes its air!''

Strait *Lydia* smil'd; the comb adjusts her locks;
And at the Play-house, *Harry* keeps her box.

SATURDAY.

THE SMALL-POX.

FLAVIA.

THE wretched *Flavia* on her couch reclin'd,
Thus breath'd the anguish of a wounded mind,
A glass revers'd in her right hand she bore,
For now she shun'd the face she sought before.
„ How am I chang'd! alas! how am I grown
„ A frightful spectre, to myself unknown!
„ Where's my complexion? where my radiant bloom,
„ That promis'd happiness for years to come?

„Then with what pleasure I this face
　　　survey'd!
„To look once more, my visits oft de-
　　　lay'd!
„Charm'd with the view, a fresher red
　　　would rise,
„And a new life shot sparkling from
　　　my eyes!
„Ah! faithless glass, my wonted bloom
　　　restore;
„Alas! I rave, that bloom is now no
　　　more;
„The greatest good the gods on men
　　　bestow,
„Ev'n youth itself to me is useless now.
„There was a time (oh! that I could
　　　forget!)
„When opera-tickets pour'd before my
　　　feet;
„And at the ring, where brightest beau-
　　　ties shine,
„The earliest cherries of the spring were
　　　mine.

,, Witness, O Lilly; and thou, Motteux,
tell,
,, How much japan these eyes have made
ye fell.
,, With what contempt ye saw me oft
despise
,, The humble offer of the raffled prize;
,, For at the raffle still each prize I bore,
,, With scorn rejected, or with triumph
wore!
,, Now beauty's fled, and presents are
no more!
,, For me the Patriot has the house
forsook,
,, And left debates to catch a passing look:
,, For me the soldier has soft verses writ:
,, For me the beau has aim'd to be a wit.
,, For me the Wit to nonsense was
betray'd;
,, The Gamester has for me his dun de-
lay'd,
,, And overseen the card he would have
play'd.

„ The bold and haughty by succefs made
vain,
„ Aw'd by my eyes, have trembled to
complain;
„ The bashful 'Squire touch'd by a wish
unknown,
„ Has dar'd to speak with spirit not his
own:
„ Fir'd by one wish, all did alike adore;
„ Now beauty's fled, and lovers are no
more!
„ As round the room I turn my weep-
ing eyes,
„ New unaffected scenes of sorrow rise.
„ Far from my sight that killing picture
bear,
„ The face disfigure, and the canvafs tear:
„ That picture, which with pride I us'd
to shew,
„ The lost resemblance but upbraids me
now.
„ And thou, my toilette! where I oft
have sate,

„ While hours unheeded pafs'd in deep
debate,
„ How curls fhould fall, or where a patch
to place;
„ If blue or fcarlet beft became my face;
„ Now on fome happier nymph your aid
beftow;
„ On fairer heads, ye ufelefs jewels,
glow!
„ No borrow'd luftre can my charms
reftore;
„ Beauty is fled, and drefs is now no
more!
„ Ye meaner beauties, I permit ye
fhine;
„ Go, triumph in the hearts that once
were mine.
„ But 'midft your triumphs with confufion
know,
„ 'Tis to my ruin all your arms ye owe.
„ Would pitying heav'n reftore my wont-
ed mien,
„ Ye ftill might move unthought of and
unfeen:

„But oh, how vain, how wretched is
      the boaſt
„Of beauty faded, and of empire loſt!
„What now is left but weeping, to
      deplore
„My beauty fled, and empire now no
      more?
„Ye cruel chymiſts, what withheld
      your aid!
„Could no pomatums ſave a trembling
      maid?
„How falſe and trifling is that art ye
      boaſt!
„No art can give me back my beauty loſt.
„In tears, ſurrounded by my friends I lay,
„Maſk'd o'er, and trembled at the ſight
      of day;
„*Mirmillo* came my fortune to deplore,
„(A golden-headed cane well carv'd he
      bore)
„Cordials, he cry'd, my ſpirits muſt
      reſtore!
„Beauty is fled, and ſpirit is no more!

„ *Galen*, the grave; officious *Squirt*,
            was there;
„ With fruitless grief and unavailing care:
„ *Machaon* too, the great *Machaon*,
            known,
„ By his red cloak and his superior frown;
„ And why, he cry'd, this grief and this
            despair,
„ You shall again be well, again be fair;
„ Believe my oath; (with that an oath
            he swore)
„ False was his oath; my beauty is no
            more!
„ Cease, hapless maid, no more thy
            tale pursue.
„ Forsake mankind, and bid the world
            adieu!
„ Monarchs and beauties rule with equal
            sway;
„ All strive to serve, and glory to obey:
„ Alike unpitied when depos'd they
            grow—
„ Men mock the idol of their former vow.

„Adieu! ye parks!—in some obscure recess,
„Where gentle streams will weep at my distress,
„Where no false friend will in my grief take part,
„And mourn my ruin with a joyful heart;
„There let me live in some deserted place,
„There hide in shades this lost inglorious face.
„Plays, operas, circles, I no more must view!
„My toilette, patches, all the world adieu!"

VERSES *)

Addressed to the

IMITATOR

Of the FIRST SATIRE of the

Second Book of *HORACE.*

In two large columns on thy motly page,
Where Roman wit is stripe'd with English rage;

---

*) These severe Verses owe their birth to two lines in the first Satire of the Second Book of Horace, imitated by Mr. Pope, which were supposed to point at Lady Mary Wortley Montague, under the name of Sappho. We find by the Letters of Mr. Pope, vol. 7. and those of Lady Mary Wortley Montague lately published, that a friendly correspondence once subsisted

Where ribaldry to fatire makes pretence,
And modern fcandal rolls with ancient
fenfe:

between thefe two Wits, which probably did not continue much later than her ladyfhip's return into England in the year 1718. But the exact time when the quarrel between them commenced, and the circumftances relating to it, are not eafy, at this diftance of time, to difcover. It is faid in Mr. Pope's Life, (Biographia Britannica, vol. 5. p. 3413) that he was charged with propagating a fcandalous report concerning her ladyfhip, which, it is added, perhaps he was not quite clear of. The note to that life in which this charge on the poet is to he found, has the name of Dr. Warburton annexed to it, and therefore, on his authority, may well be fuppofed not without foundation. If a conjecture may be allowed, it is not improbable that this was the occafion of their difference. With refpect to the lines which produced thefe verfes, Mr. Pope, in his letter to Lord Hervey, vol. 8. p. 196. abfolutely difclaims any inten-

Whilst on one side we see how Horace
 thought,
And on the other how he never wrote:

tion of applying them to Lady Montague
„ In regard (says he) to the right honour-
„ able Lady, your Lordship's friend, I was
„ far from designing a person of her con-
„ dition by a name so derogatory to her
„ as that of Sappho, a name prostituted
„ to every infamous creature that ever
„ wrote verse or novels. I protest I never
„ applied that name to her in any verse
„ of mine, public or private, and (I firmly
„ believe) not in any letter or conver-
„ sation." What degree of credit this asseve-
ration deserves must be left to the reader's
determination, only observing, that Mr.
Pope was not very scrupulous in disowning
a character when the opinion of the Public
was not in his favour. With equal, or
more earnestness, he denied that the description of Timon's Villa was designed
to expose that of a certain nobleman. In
which particular, he has been unwarily
given up by his Commentator, who, in
the following note on these lines in the

Who can believe, who view the bad
and good,
That the dull copift better underftood

edition of 1751, feems to acknowledge the fact.

Another age fhall fee the golden car
Imbrown the flope, and nod on the
parterre;
Deep harvefts bury all his pride had
plann'd,
And laughing Ceres re-affume the land.
MORAL EPISTLES iv. Verfe 172.

,, Had the poet lived but three years ,, longer, he had feen this prophecy ful- ,, filled." It is to be remembered, that Canons was fold about the time here fixed upon, and therefore this queftion will naturally arife, What prophecy was fulfilled, if Mr. Pope had not that place in his mind while he was writing the before mentioned Epiftle? The Editor of his works, as if confcious that he had done no fervice to Mr. Pope's moral character, by the above note, has fince altered it in the

S 3

That Spirit, he pretends to imitate,
Than heretofore that Greek he did tranſlate?
Thine is juſt ſuch an image of *his* pen,
As thou thyſelf art of the ſons of men:
Where our own ſpecies in burleſque we trace,
A ſign-poſt likeneſs of the human race;
That is' at once reſemblance and diſgrace.
Horace can laugh, is delicate, is clear;
You only coarſely rail, or darkly ſneer:
His ſtyle is elegant, his diction pure,
Whilſt none thy crabbed numbers can endure;
Hard as thy heart, and as thy birth obſcure.
If *he* has thorns, they all on roſes grow;

following manner: „ Had the poet lived „ three years longer he had ſeen his gene- „ ral prophecy *againſt all ill-judged mag- „ nificence fulfilled in a very particular „ inſtance.*"

Thine like rude thistles, and mean
            brambles show,
With this exception, that tho' rank the soil,
Weeds as they are they seem produc'd
            by toil.
Satire should, like a polish'd razor keen,
Wound with a touch, that's scarcely
            felt or seen.
Thine is an oyster-knife, that hacks
            and hews;
The rage, but not the talent to abuse;
And is in *hate*, what *love* is in the
            stews.
'Tis the gross *lust* of hate, that still
            annoys,
Without distinction, as gross love enjoys:
Neither to folly, nor to vice confin'd;
The object of thy spleen is human kind:
It preys on all, who yield or who resist:
To thee 'tis provocation to exist.

But if thou feest *) a great and gene-
            -rous heart,

*) See *Taste*, an Epistle.

Thy bow is doubly bent to force a dart.
Nor dignity nor innocence is spar'd,
Nor age, nor sex, nor thrones, nor graves
 rever'd.
Nor only justice vainly we demand,
But even benefits can't rein thy hand:
To this or that alike in vain we trust,
Nor find thee less ungrateful than unjust.
 Not even youth and beauty can con-
 troul
The universal rancour of thy soul;
Charms that might soften superstition's
 rage,
Might humble pride, or thaw the ice
 of age.
But how should'st thou by beauty's force
 be mov'd,
No more for loving made, than to be
 lov'd?
It was the equity of righteous heav'n,
That such a soul to such a form was
 giv'n;
And shews the uniformity of fate,

That one so odious should be born to hate.
  When God created thee, one would
          believe,
He said the same as to the snake of *Eve*:
To human race antipathy declare,
'Twixt them and thee be everlasting war.
But oh! the sequel of the sentence dread,
And whilst you *bruise their heel*, be-
       ware your head.
  Nor think thy weakness shall be thy
         defence;
The female scold's protection in offence.
Sure 'tis as fair to beat who cannot fight,
As 'tis to libel those who cannot write.
And if thou draw'st thy pen to aid the law,
Others a cudgel, or a rod, may draw.
If none with vengeance yet thy crimes
        pursue,
Or give thy manifold affronts their due;
If limbs unbroken, skin without a stain,
Unwhipt, unblanketed, unkick'd, un-
        slain;
That wretched little carcase you retain:

The reason is, not that the world wants
eyes;
But thou'rt so mean, they see, and they
despise:
When fretful *porcupine*, with raucorous
will,
From mounted back shoots forth a harm-
less quill,
Cool the spectators stand, and all the
while,
Upon the angry little monster smile.
Thus 'tis with thee:—while impotently
safe,
You strike unwounding, we unhurt can
laugh.
*Who but must laugh, this bully when
he sees,*
A puny insect shiv'ring at a breeze?
One over-match'd by ev'ry blast of wind,
Insulting and provoking all mankind.
Is this the *thing* to keep mankind in
awe,
*To make those tremble who escape the
law?*

Is this *the ridicule* to live so long,
The *deathless satire*, and *immortal*
Song?
No: like thy self-blown praise, thy scan-
dal flies;
And, as we're told of wasps, it stings
and dies.
If none do yet return th' intended blow,
You all your safety to your dullness owe:
But whilst that armour thy poor corps
defends,
'Twill make thy readers few, as are thy
friends;
Those, who thy nature loath'd yet lov'd
thy art,
Who lik'd thy head, and yet abhorr'd
thy heart;
Chose thee, to read, but never to con-
verse,
And scorn'd in prose, him whom they
priz'd in verse.
Even they shall now their partial error
see,

Shall shun thy writings like thy company;
And to thy books shall ope their eyes
no more,
Than to thy person they would do their
door.
Nor thou the justice of the world
disown,
That leaves thee thus an out-cast, and
alone;
For tho' in law, to murder be to kill,
In equity the murder's in the will:
Then whilst with coward hand you stab
a name,
And try at least t'assassinate our fame;
Like the first bold assassins be thy lot,
Ne'er be thy guilt forgiven, or forgot;
But as thou hat'st, be hated by mankind,
And with the emblem of thy crooked
mind,
Mark'd on thy back, like Cain, by
God's own hand,
Wander, like him, accursed through
the land.

AN EPISTLE

TO

LORD B——.

How happy you! who varied joys
        pursue;
And every hour presents you something
        new!
Plans, schemes, and models, all Pal-
        ladio's art,
For six long months have gain'd upon
        your heart;
Of colonnades, of corridores you talk,
The winding stair-case and the cover'd
        walk;
You blend the orders with Vitruvian toil,
And raise with wond'rous joy the fancy'd
        pile;
But the dull workman's slow performing
        hand

But coldly executes his lord's command.
With dirt and mortar foon you go dif-
pleas'd,
Planting fucceeds, and avenues are rais'd,
Canals are cut, and mountains level
made;
Bowers of retreat, and galleries of fhade;
The fhaven turf prefents a lively green;
The bordering flowers in myftic knots
are feen;
With ftudied art on nature you refine— —
The fpring beheld you warm in this
defign,
But fcarce the cold attacks your fav'rite
trees,
Your inclination fails, and wifhes freeze;
You quit the grove, fo lately you ad-
mir'd;
With other views your eager hopes are
fir'd.
Poft to the city you direct your way;
Not blooming paradife could bribe your
ftay;

Ambition shews you power's brightest
           side,
'Tis meanly poor in solitude to hide:
Though certain pains attend the care of
           state,
A good man owes his country to be great;
Shou'd act abroad the high-distinguish'd
           part,
Or shew at least the purpose of his heart.
With thoughts like these the shining
           courts you seek:
Full of new projects for almost a week:
You then despise the tinsel glittering
           snare,
Think vile mankind below a serious care.
Life is too short for any distant aim,
And cold the dull reward of future fame.
Be happy then, while yet you have to
           live;
And love is all the blessing heav'n can
           give.
Fir'd by new passion you address the
           fair;

Survey the opera as a gay parterre:
Young Cloe's bloom had made you cer-
   tain prize,
But for a side-long glance from Celia's
   eyes:
Your beating heart acknowledges her
   power;
Your eager eyes her lovely form devour;
You feel the poison swelling in your
   breast,
And all your soul by fond desire possess'd.
In dying sighs a long three hours are
   past;
To some assembly with impatient haste,
With trembling hope, and doubtful fear
   you move,
Resolv'd to tempt your fate, and own
   your love:
But there Belinda meets you on the stairs,
Easy her shape, attracting all her airs;
A smile she gives, and with a smile can
   wound;
Her melting voice has music in the sound;

Her every motion wears refiftlefs grace;
Wit in her mien, and pleafure in her face:
Here while you vow eternity of love,
Cloe and Celia unregarded move.
  Thus on the fands of Afric's burning plains,
However deeply made, no long imprefs remains;
The flighteft leaf can leave its figure there;
The ftrongeft form is fcattered by the air.
So yielding the warm temper of your mind;
So touch'd by every eye, fo tofs'd by wind;
Oh! how unlike the heav'n my foul defign'd!
Unfeen, unheard, the throng around me move;
Not wifhing praife; infenfible of love:
No whifpers foften, nor no beauties fire;
Carelefs I fee the dance, and coldly hear the lyre.

So num'rous herds are driv'n o'er the
   rock;
No print is left of all the passing flock:
So sings the wind around the solid stone,
So vainly beat the waves with fruitless
   moan
Tedious the toil, and great the work-
   man's care,
Who dare attempt to fix impressions
   there:
But should some swain more skilful than
   the rest,
Engrave his name upon this marble breast,
Not rolling ages could deface that name;
Thro' all the storms of life 'tis still the
   same:
Tho' length of years with moss may shade
   the ground,
Deep, though unseen, remains the secret
   wound.

EPISTLE

FROM

ARTHUR GREY, the Footman *),

After his Condemnation for attempting a *Rape*.

READ, lovely nymph, and tremble
    not to read,
I have no more to wish, nor you to
    dread:

---

*) This man was footman to a gentleman, whose daughter, a married lady, he attempted to ravish. It appears by his trial, that he went into her room about four o'clock in the morning, armed with a pistol in one hand, and a drawn sword in the other; and advancing to the bedside, threatened to murder her if she made any noise. Upon asking him what he meant by coming into her chamber in such a manner, he replied, that he intended to ravish her, for that he had entertained a violent love for her a long time; but as

I aſk not life, for life to me were vain,
And death a refuge from ſeverer pain.
My only hope in theſe laſt lines I try,
I would be pitied, and I then would
die.

Long had I liv'd as ſordid as my
fate,
Nor curs'd the deſtiny that made me wait
A ſervile ſlave: content with homely
food,
The groſs inſtinct of happineſs purſu'd:
Youth gave me ſleep at night, and
warmth of blood.

there was ſo great a difference between their fortunes, he deſpaired of enjoying his wiſhes by any means but force. After ſome reſiſtence, the lady wrenched the piſtol from his hand, (he having laid down the ſword) and rung the bell; upon which he ran away. He was indicted and convicted of a burglary, at the Old Bailey in December 1721, but the ſentence was not executed, for he was reprieved, and afterwards tranſported.

Ambition yet had never touch'd my
   breaſt;
My lordly maſter knew no ſounder reſt;
With labour healthy, in obedience bleſt.
But when I ſaw——oh! had I never ſeen
That wounding ſoftneſs, that engaging
   mien!
The miſt of wretched education flies,
Shame, fear, deſire, deſpair and love
   ariſe,
The new creation of thoſe beauteous
   eyes.
But yet that love purſu'd no guilty aim,
Deep in my heart I hid the ſecret flame.
I never hop'd my fond deſire to tell;
And all my wiſhes were to ſerve you
   well.
Heav'ns! how I flew, when wing'd by
   your command,
And kiſs'd the letters giv'n me by your
   hand!
How pleas'd, how proud, how fond was
   I to wait,

Present the sparkling wine, or change
 the plate!
How when you sung my soul devour'd
 the sound,
And ev'ry sense was in the rapture
 drown'd!
Tho' bid to go, I quite forgot to move;
——You knew not that stupidity was
 love!
But oh! the torment not to be express'd,
The grief, the rage, the hell that fir'd
 this breast,
When my great rivals, in embroid'ry gay,
Sate by your side, or led you from the
 play!
I still contriv'd near as I could to stand,
(The flambeau trembling in my shaking
 hand)
I saw, or thought I saw, those fingers
 press'd,
For thus their passion by my own I
 guess'd,
And jealous fury all my soul possess'd.

Like torrents, love and indignation meet,
And madness would have thrown me at
your feet.
Turn, lovely nymph, (for so I would
have said)
Turn from those triflers who make love
a trade;
This is true passion in my eyes you see;
They cannot, no— —they cannot love
like me.
Frequent debauch has pall'd their sickly
taste,
Faint their desire, and in a moment
past:
They sigh not from the heart, but from
the brain;
Vapours of vanity, and strong cham-
pagne.
Too dull to feel what forms, like yours,
inspire,
After long talking of their painted fire,
To some lewd brothel they at night re-
tire;

There pleas'd with fancy'd quality and
  charms,
Enjoy your beauties in a ſtrumpet's
  arms.
Such are the joys thoſe toaſters have
  in view,
And ſuch the wit and pleaſure they
  purſue:
——And is this love that ought to
  merit you?

Each opera-night a new addreſs begun,
They ſwear to thouſands what they
  ſwear to one.
Not thus I ſigh—but all my ſighs are
  vain—
Die, wretched *Arthur*, and conceal
  thy pain:
'Tis impudence to wiſh, and madneſs
  to complain.

  Fix'd on this view, my only hope of
  eaſe,
I waited not the aid of ſlow diſeaſe:
The keeneſt inſtruments of death I ſought,

And death alone employ'd my lab'ring
thought.
This all the night—when I remember
well,
The charming tinkle of your morning
bell!
Fir'd by the found, I haften'd with your
tea,
With one laft look to fmooth the dark-
fome way.—
But oh! how dear that fatal look has coft!
In that fond moment my refolves were
loft.
Hence all my guilt, and all your for-
rows rife—
I faw the languid foftnefs of your eyes;
I faw the dear diforder of your bed;
Your cheeks all glowing with a tempt-
ing red;
Your night-cloaths tumbled with refift-
lefs grace;
Your flowing hair play'd carelefs down
your face,

Your night-gown faſten'd with a ſingle
pin;
—Fancy improv'd the wond'rous charms
within!
I fix'd my eyes upon that heaving
breaſt,
And hardly, hardly I forbore the reſt;
Eager to gaze, unſatisfy'd with ſight,
My head grew giddy with the near
delight!
—Too well you know the fatal fol-
lowing night!
Th' extremeſt proof of my deſire I give,
And ſince you will not love, I will not
live.
Condemn'd by you, I wait the righteous
doom,
Careleſs and fearleſs of the woes to
come.
But when you ſee me waver in the
wind,
My guilty flame extinct, my ſoul re-
ſgn'd,

Sure you may pity what you can't ap-
    prove,
The cruel confequence of furious love.
Think the bold wretch, that could fo
    greatly dare,
Was tender, faithful, ardent, and fincere:
Think when I held the piftol to your
    breaft,
Had I been of the world's large rule
    poffefs'd,
That world had then been yours, and
    I been bleft!
Think that my life was quite below my
    care,
Nor fear'd I any hell beyond defpair.——
  If thefe reflections, though they feize
    you late,
Give fome compaffion for your *Arthur's*
    fate:
Enough you give, nor ought I to com-
    plain;
You pay my pangs, nor have I dy'd
    in vain.

AN ANSWER TO A LOVE-LETTER.

Is it to me, this sad lamenting strain?
Are heaven's choicest gifts bestow'd in vain?
A plenteous fortune, and a beauteous bride,
Your love rewarded, gratify'd your pride:
Yet leaving her——'tis me that you pursue
Without one single charm, but being new.
How vile is man! how I detest their ways
Of artful falshood, and designing praise!
Tasteless, an easy happiness you slight,
Ruin your joy, and mischief your delight.

Why should poor pug (the mimic of
    your kind)
Wear a rough chain, and be to box
    confin'd?
Some cup, perhaps he breaks, or tears
    a fan,———
While roves unpunish'd the destroyer,
    man.
Not bound by vows, and unrestrain'd
    by shame,
In sport you break the heart, and rend
    the same.
Not that your art can be successful here,
Th' already plunder'd need no robber
    fear:
Nor sighs, nor charms, nor flatteries
    can move,
Too well secur'd against a second love.
Once, and but once, that devil charm'd
    my mind;
To reason deaf, to observation blind;
I idly hop'd (what cannot love per-
    suade!)

U 3

My fondness equal'd, and my love re-
	pay'd;
Slow to distrust, and willing to be-
	lieve,
Long hush'd my doubts, and did my-
	self deceive:
But oh! too soon— —this tale would
	ever last;
Sleep, sleep my wrongs, and let me
	think 'em past.
For you, who mourn with counterfeit-
	ed grief,
And ask so boldly like a begging thief,
May soon some other nymph inflict the
	pain,
You know so well with cruel art to
	feign.
Tho' long you sported have with Cu-
	pid's dart,
You may see eyes, and you may feel
	a heart.
So the brisk wits, who flop the evening
	coach,

Laugh at the fear which follows their
 approach;
With idle mirth, and haughty scorn
 despise
The passenger's pale cheek, and staring
 eyes:
But seiz'd by Justice, find a fright no
 jest,
And all the terror doubled in their breast.

AN
ELEGY
on
Mrs. THOMPSON.

UNHAPPY fair! by fatal love betray'd!
Must then thy beauties thus untimely
 fade?
And all thy blooming, soft, inspiring
 charms,

Become a prey to death's destructive
	arms?
Tho' short thy day, and transient like
	the wind,
How far more bless than those yet left
	behind!
Safe in the grave, thy griefs with thee
	remain,
And life's tempestuous billows break in
	vain.
Ye tender nymphs in lawless pastimes gay,
Who heedless down the paths of plea-
	sure stray,
Tho' long secure, with blissful joy elate,
Yet pause, and think of Arabella's fate:
For such may be your unexpected doom,
And your next slumbers lull you in the
	tomb.
But let it be the muse's gentle care
To shield from envy's rage the mould'ring
	fair;
To draw a veil o'er faults she can't
	defend;

And what prudes have devour'd, leave
    time to end:
Be it her part to drop a pitying tear,
And mourning sigh around thy sable bier.
Nor shall thy woes long glad th' ill-
    natur'd crowd,
Silent to praise, and in detraction loud:
When scandal, that thro' life each worth
    destroys,
And malice that imbitters all our joys,
Shall in some ill starr'd wretch find lat-
    er stains;
And let thine rest, forgot as thy re-
    mains.

IN ANSWER TO A LADY,

WHO

ADVISED RETIREMENT.

YOU little know the heart that you
    advise;
I view this various scene with equal eyes;

In crowded courts I find myself alone,
And pay my worship to a nobler throne.
Long since the value of this world I know,
Pity the madness, and despise the show:
Well as I can my tedious part I bear,
And wait for my dismission without fear.
Seldom I mark mankind's detested ways,
Not hearing censure, nor affecting praise;
And, unconcern'd, my future state I trust
To that sole Being, merciful and just.

ON THE

DEATH

OF

Mrs. *BOWES.*

Written extempore on a card, in a great deal of company, Dec. 14. 1724.

HAIL happy bride, for thou art truly
    blest!
Three months of rapture, crown'd with
    endless rest.

Merit, like yours, was heaven's peculiar
    care,
You lov'd—yet tasted happiness sincere.
To you the sweets of love were only
    shewn,
The sure succeeding bitter dregs unknown;
You had not yet the fatal change deplor'd,
The tender lover, for the imperious lord:
Nor felt the pain that jealous fondness
    brings;
Nor felt the coldness, from possession
    springs.
Above your sex, distinguish'd in your fate,
You trusted—yet experienced no deceit;
Soft were your hours, and wing'd with
    pleasure flew;
No vain repentance gave a sigh to you:
And if superior bliss heaven can bestow,
With fellow angels you enjoy it now.

VERSES
Written in a GARDEN.

SEE how that pair of billing doves
With open murmurs own their loves;
And heedless of censorious eyes,
Pursue their unpolluted joys:
No fears of future want molest
The downy quiet of their nest;
No int'rest join'd the happy pair,
Securely bless in Nature's care,
While her dear dictates they pursue:
For constancy is nature too.

 Can all the doctrine of our schools,
Our maxims, our religious rules,
Can learning to our lives ensure
Virtue so bright, or bliss so pure?
The great Creator's happy ends,
Virtue and pleasure ever blends:
In vain the church and court have try'd
Th' united essence to divide;
Alike they find their wild mistake,
The pedant priest, and giddy rake.

A HYMN
TO THE
MOON.

Written in July, in an Arbour.

Thou silver Deity of secret night,
  Direct my footsteps thro' the woodland shade;
Thou conscious witness of unknown delight,
  The lover's guardian, and the muses' aid!
By thy pale beams I solitary rove,
  To thee my tender grief confide;
Serenely sweet you gild the silent grove,
  My friend, my goddess, and my guide.
E'en thee, fair queen, from thy amazing height,
  The charms of young Endymion drew;
Veil'd with the mantle of concealing night;
  With all thy greatness, and thy coldness too.

EPILOGUE*)

TO

MARY, Queen of SCOTS.

Design'd to be spoken by Mrs. OLDFIELD.

WHAT could luxurious woman wiſh
  for more,
To fix her joys, or to extend her pow'r?
Their every wiſh was in this Mary ſeen,

---

*) This Epilogue was intended for a Play on the Story of Mary Queen of Scots, which the Duke of Wharton began to write, but never finiſhed. No part of the Play now remains, but theſe four lines:

Sure were I free, and Norfolk were a
  priſoner,
I'd fly with more impatience to his arms,
Than the poor Iſraelite gaz'd on the
  ſerpent,
When life was the reward of every look.

Walpole's Catalogue, vol. II. p. 134.

Gay, witty, youthful, beauteous, and
a queen.
Vain useless blessings with ill conduct
join'd!
Light as the air, and fleeting as the wind,
Whatever poets write, and lovers vow,
Beauty, what poor omnipotence hast
thou!
Queen Bess had wisdom, council,
power, and laws;
How few espous'd a wretched beauty's
cause!
Learn thence, ye fair, more solid charms
to prize,
Contemn the idle flatt'rers of your eyes.
The brightest object shines but while 'tis
new:
That influence lessens by familiar view.
Monarchs and beauties rule with equal
sway,
All strive to serve, and glory to obey;
Alike unpitied when depos'd they grow—
Men mock the idol of their former vow.

Two great examples have been shewn
  to-day,
To what sure ruin passion does betray;
What long repentance to short joys is due;
When reason rules, what glory does
  ensue.
If you will love, love like Eliza then;
Love for amusement, like those traitors,
  men.
Think that the pastime of a leisure hour
She favour'd oft—but never shar'd her
  pow'r.
The traveller by desart wolves pursu'd,
If by his art the savage foe's subdu'd,
The world will still the noble act ap-
  plaud,
Tho' victory was gain'd by needful fraud.
Such is, my tender sex, our helpless
  case;
And such the barbarous heart, hid by
  the begging face.
By passion fir'd, and not withheld by
  shame,

They cruel hunters are; we, trembling
  game.
Trust me, dear ladies, (for I know 'em
  well)
They burn to triumph, and they sigh
  to tell:
Cruel to them to yield, cullies to them
  that fell.
Believe me, 'tis by far the wiser course,
Superior art should meet superior force:
Hear, but be faithful to your int'rest still:
Secure your hearts—then fool with whom
  you will.

A BALLAD.

To the Tune of, *The Irish Howl.*

To that dear nymph, whose powerful
  name
Does every throbbing nerve inflame,
(As the soft sound I low repeat
My pulse unequal measures beat)

Whose eyes I never more shall see,
That once so sweetly shin'd on thee;
Go, gentle wind! and kindly bear
My tender wishes to the fair.
     Hoh, ho, ho, etc.

Amidst her pleasures let her know
The secret anguish of my woe,
The midnight pang, the jealous hell,
Does in this tortur'd bosom dwell:
While laughing she, and full of play,
Is with her young companions gay;
Or hearing in some fragrant bower
Her lover's sigh, and beauty's power.
     Hoh, ho, ho, etc.

Lost and forgotten may I be!
Oh may no pitying thought of me
Disturb the joy that she may find,
When love is crown'd, and fortune kind:
May that bless'd swain (whom yet I hate)
Be proud of his distinguish'd fate;
Each happy night be like the first,
And he be bless'd as I am curs'd.
     Hoh, ho, ho, etc.

While in these pathless woods I stray,
And lose my solitary way,
Talk to the stars, to trees complain,
And tell the senseless woods my pain:
But madness spares the sacred name,
Nor dares the hidden wound proclaim;
Which secret rankling, sure and slow,
Shall close in endless peace my woe.
      - Hoh, ho, ho, etc.
When this fond heart shall ake no
    more,
And all the ills of life are o'er;
(If gods by lovers' prayers are mov'd
As every god in heaven has lov'd)
Instead of bright Elysian joys,
That unknown something in the skies,
In recompence of all my pain,
The only heaven I would obtain,
May I the guardian of charms
Preserve that paradise from harms.
     Hoh, ho, ho, etc.

THE LOVER:
A BALLAD.
To Mr. C——.

At length, by so much importunity press'd,
Take, C—, at once the inside of my breast.
This stupid indiff'rence so often you blame,
Is not owing to nature, to fear, or to shame:
I am not as cold as a virgin in lead,
Nor is Sunday's sermon so strong in my head:
I know but too well how time flies along,
That we live but few years, and yet fewer are young.

But I hate to be cheated, and never will buy
Long years of repentance for moments of joy.

Oh! was there a man (but where shall
 I find
Good sense and good nature so equally
 join'd?)
Would value his pleasure, contribute
 to mine;
Not meanly would boast, nor lewdly
 design,
Not over severe, yet not stupidly vain,
For I would have the power, tho' not
 give the pain.

No pedant, yet learned; no rake-helly
 gay,
Or laughing, because he has nothing
 to say;
To all my whole sex, obliging and free,
Yet never be fond of any but me;
In public preserve the decorum that's just,
And shew in his eyes he is true to his trust;
Then rarely approach, and respectfully
 bow,
But not fulsomely pert, nor foppishly
 low.

But when the long hours of public are
paſt,
And we meet with champagne and a
chicken at laſt,
May every fond pleaſure that moment
endear;
Be baniſh'd afar both diſcretion and fear!
Forgetting or ſcorning the airs of the
crowd,
He may ceaſe to be formal, and I to be
proud,
'Till loſt in the joy, we confeſs that we
live,
And he may be rude, and yet I may
forgive.

And that my delight may be ſolidly
fix'd,
Let the friend and the lover be hand-
ſomely mix'd,
In whoſe tender boſom my ſoul may
confide,
Whoſe kindneſs can ſooth me, whoſe
counſel can guide.

From such a dear lover as here I describe,
No danger should fright me, no millions
   should bribe;
But till this astonishing creature I know,
As I long have liv'd chaste, I will keep
   myself so.

I never will share with the wanton
   coquet,
Or be caught by a vain affectation of wit.
The toasters and songsters may try all
   their art,
But never shall enter the pass of my heart.
I loath the lewd rake, the dress'd fopling
   despise:
Before such pursuers the nice virgin flies:
And as OVID has sweetly in parable told,
We harden like trees, and like rivers
   grow cold.

THE LADY's RESOLVE.

Written extempore on a Window.

WHILST thirst of praise, and vain
desire of fame,
In every age, is every woman's aim;
With courtship pleas'd, of silly toasters
proud,
Fond of a train, and happy in a crowd;
On each poor fool bestowing some kind
glance,
Each conquest owing to some loose ad-
vance;
While vain coquets affect to be pursu'd,
And think they're virtuous, if not grosly
lewd :.
Let this great maxim be my virtue's
guide;
In part she is to blame that has been
try'd—
He comes too near that comes to be
deny'd.

THE GENTLEMAN's ANSWER.

WHILST pretty fellows think a woman's fame
In ev'ry state and ev'ry age the same;
With their own folly pleas'd, the fair they toast,
And where they least are happy, swear they're most;
No difference making 'twixt coquet and prude;
And her that seems, yet is not really lewd;
While thus they think, and thus they vainly live,
And taste no joys but what their fancy give;
Let this great maxim be my action's guide:
May I ne'er hope, though I am ne'er deny'd;
Nor think a woman won, that's willing to be try'd.

A MAN in LOVE.

*L'Homme qui ne se trouve point et
ne se trouvera jamais.*

THE man who feels the dear disease,
Forgets himself, neglects to please;
The crowd avoids and seeks the groves,
And much he thinks when much he
     loves;
Press'd with alternate hope and fear,
Sighs in her absence, sighs when she is
    near.
The gay, the fond, the fair, the young,
Those trifles pass unseen along,
To him a pert, insipid throng.
But most he shuns the vain coquet;
Contemns her false affected wit:
The minstrels sound, the flowing bowl,
Oppress and hurt the am'rous soul.
'Tis solitude alone can please,
And give some intervals of ease.
He feeds the soft distemper there,

And fondly courts the distant fair;
To balls, the silent shade prefers;
And hates all other charms but hers.
When thus your absent swain can do,
Molly, you may believe him true.

A RECEIPT To cure the VAPOURS.

Written to Lady J——N.

WHY will Delia thus retire,
  And idly languish life away?
While the fighing crowd admire,
  'Tis too soon for hartshorn tea.

All those dismal looks and fretting
  Cannot Damon's life restore;
Long ago the worms have eat him,
  You can never see him more.

Once again confult your toilette,
 In the glafs your face review:
So much weeping foon will fpoil it,
 And no fpring your charms renew.

I, like you, was born a woman,
 Well I know what vapours mean:
The difeafe, alas! is common;
 Single, we have all the fpleen.

All the morals that they tell us,
 Never cur'd the forrow yet:
Chufe, among the pretty fellows,
 One of honour, youth, and wit.

Prithee hear him every morning,
 At the leaft an hour or two;
Once again at night returning—
 I believe the dofe will do.

THE FIFTH ODE OF HORACE
IMITATED.

For whom are now your airs put on,
And what new beauty's doom'd to be
undone?
That careless elegance of dress,
This essence that perfumes the wind,
Your very motion does confess
Some secret conquest is design'd.
Alas! the poor unhappy maid,
To what a train of ills betray'd!
What fears, what pangs shall rend
her breast!
How will her eyes dissolve in tears!
That now with glowing joy is bless'd,
Charm'd with the faithless vows she
hears.
So the young sailor on the summer sea,
Gaily pursues his destin'd way:
Fearless and careless on the deck
he stands,

Till sudden storms arise and thunders
   roll;
In vain he casts his eyes to distant
   lands,
Distracting terror tears his timorous soul.
For me, secure I view the raging main,
Past are my dangers, and forgot my pain:
 My votive tablet in the temple shews
  The monument of folly past;
  I paid the bounteous god my grate-
   ful vows,
 Who snatch'd from ruin, sav'd me at
   the last.

FAREWELL TO BATH.

To all you ladies now at Bath,
 And eke, ye beaus, to you,
With aking heart, and watry eyes,
 I bid my last adieu.

Farewell ye nymphs, who waters sip
 Hot reeking from the pumps,

While music lends her friendly aid,
  To cheer you from the dumps.

Farewell, ye wits, who prating stand,
  And criticife the fair;
Yourfelves the joke of men of fenfe,
  Who hate a coxcomb's air.

Farewell to Deard's, and all her toys,
  Which glitter in her fhop,
Deluding traps to girls and boys,
  The warehoufe of the fop.

Lindfay's and Hayes's both farewell,
  Where in the fpacious hall,
With bounding fteps, and fprightly air,
  I've led up many a ball.

Where Somerville of courteous mein,
  Was partner in the dance,
With fwimming Haws, and Brownlow
        blithe,
  And Britton pink of France.

Poor Nash, farewell! may fortune smile,
   Thy drooping soul revive,
My heart is full, I can no more—
   John, bid the Coachman drive.

TO CLIO.

Occasioned by her Verses on
FRIENDSHIP.

WHILE, Clio, pondering o'er thy lines I roll,
Dwell on each thought, and meditate thy soul,
Methinks I view thee, in some calm retreat,
Far from all guilt, distraction and deceit;
Thence pitying view, the thoughtless fair and gay,
Who whirl their lives in giddiness away;
Thence greatly scorning what the world calls great,

Contemn the proud, their tumults, pow-
er and state;
And deem it thence inglorious to de-
scend
For ought below, but virtue and a friend.
How com'st thou fram'd, so different
from thy sex,
Whom trifles ravish, and whom trifles
vex?
Capricious things, all flutter, whim and
show,
And light and varying as the winds that
blow.
To candour, sense, to love, to friendship blind,
To flatterers, fools, and coxcombs only
kind!
Say whence those hints, those bright
ideas came,
That warm thy breast with friendship's
holy flame?
That close thy heart against the joys of
youth,

And ope thy mind to all the rays of
truth?
That with such sweetness and such grace
unite,
The gay, the prudent, virtuous, and
polite?
As heaven inspires thy sentiment divine,
May heaven vouchsafe a friendship worthy
thine;
A friendship, plac'd where ease and
fragrance reign,
Where nature sways us, and no laws
restrain;
Where studious leisure, prospects unconfin'd,
And heavenly musing, lifts the aspiring
mind.
There with thy friend, may years on
years be spent,
In blooming health, and, ever gay,
content;
There blend your cares with soft assua-
sive arts,

There sooth the passions, there unfold
        your hearts;
Join in each wish, and warming into love,
Approach the raptures of the bless above.

A CAVEAT
TO THE
FAIR SEX.

WIFE and Servant are the same,
But only differ in the name;
For when that fatal knot is ty'd,
Which nothing, nothing can divide;
When she the word *obey* has said,
And man by law supreme is made:
Then all that's kind is laid aside,
And nothing left but state and pride:
Fierce as an Eastern prince he grows,
And all his innate rigour shows.
Then but to look, to laugh, to speak,
Will the nuptial contract break.
Like mutes, she signs alone must make,

And never any freedom take;
But still be govern'd by a nod,
And fear her husband as her god;
Him still must serve, him still obey,
And nothing act, and nothing say,
But what her haughty lord thinks fit,
Who with the power, has all the wit:
Then shun, O shun that wretched state,
And all the fawning flatterers hate:
Value yourselves, and men despise;
You must be proud, if you'll be wise.

End of the fifth and last Volume.

BOOKS *printed for* R. SAMMER, *Bookseller at Vienna.*

Robertson's History of the Reign of the Emperor Charles V. 4 Volumes. 8. 787.
Robertson's History of America. 3 Volumes. 8. 787.
Robertson's History of Scotland. 2 Volumes. 8. 788.
Yorick's Sentimental Journey through France and Italy. 4 Volumes. 12. 795.
The Vicar of Wakefield, a Tale by Dr. Goldsmith. 18. 796.
Pope's Essay on Man; English and German. 12. 795.
Letters betweer Yorick and Eliza; the second edition. 12. 797.
Letters of Abelard and Eloisa, with a particular account of their lives, amours and misfortunes, by John Hughes, Esq.

to which are added several Poems, by Mr. Pope and other authors. 12. 794.

The Christian's Companion; being a Choice-Manual of devout Prayers for Catholicks. 18. 795.

The Adventures of Telemachus, the Son of Ulysses, from the French of Salignac de la Mothe-Fenelon, Archbishop of Cambray; to which are added the Adventures of Aristonous. 2 Volumes. 18. 796.

Sterne's Letters to his most intimate Friends and to Eliza, together with her answers; to which is added an appendix of XXXII Letters never printed before. 2 Volumes. 12. 797.

The Man of Feeling 18 797.

Letters of Lady Mary Wortley Montague, written during her travels through Europe, Asia and Africa; to which are added by way of supplement the Poems of the same Lady. 5 Volumes. 18. 797.

Wraxall's Tour to the Northern Countries. 18. 797.

Next year will be publifhed.

The Life and Opinions of Triftram Shandy, complete in 4 Volumes. 12.
Brydone's Tour to Sicily and Malta. 2 Volumes 18.
The Adventures of Peregrine Pickle, by Dr. Smollet. 4 Volumes. 12.
Offian's Works. 4 Volumes. 12.
The Koran, by Laurence Sterne. 12.
Hamlet, a Tragedy by William Shakefpear.
Sterne's felect Works, containing his Sentimental Journey, Letters, Triftram Shandy and Koran. 8 Volumes. 12.

www.ingramcontent.com/pod-product-compliance
Lightning Source LLC
Chambersburg PA
CBHW030403250426
43670CB00050B/436